THE ASPIRING HIKER'S GUIDE 2

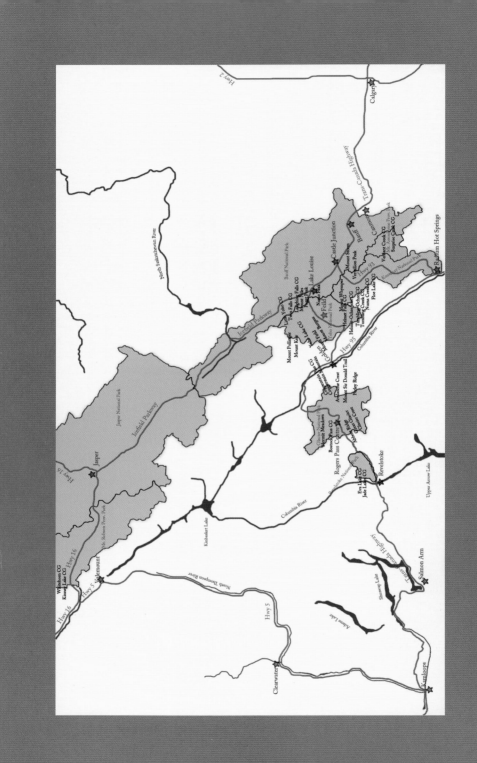

THE ASPIRING HIKER'S GUIDE 2
MOUNTAIN TREKS IN BRITISH COLUMBIA

BY GERRY SHEA, DC

RMB
Victoria Vancouver Calgary

Rocky Mountain Books
www.rmbooks.com

Library and Archives Canada Cataloguing in Publication

Shea, Gerry
 Mountain treks in British Columbia / by Gerry Shea.

(The aspiring hiker's guide ; 2)
Includes bibliographical references and index.
Issued also in an electronic format.
ISBN 978-1-926855-23-3

 1. Trails—Rocky Mountains, Canadian (B.C. and Alta.)—Guidebooks.
2. Hiking—Rocky Mountains, Canadian (B.C. and Alta.)—Guidebooks.
3. Trails—Rocky Mountains, Canadian (B.C. and Alta.)—History.
4. National parks and reserves—Rocky Mountains, Canadian (B.C. and Alta.)—Guidebooks.
5. Rocky Mountains, Canadian (B.C. and Alta.)—Guidebooks.
I. Title. II. Series: Aspiring hiker's guide ; 2

GV199.44.C22B74 2011   796.5109711'6   C2011-900285-X

Front cover photo: Looking north from Mount Kerr

Back cover photo: Surprise Creek "campground." Mount Assiniboine Provincial Park.

Printed in China

Rocky Mountain Books acknowledges the financial support for its publishing program from the Government of Canada through the Canada Book Fund (CBF) and the province of British Columbia through the British Columbia Arts Council and the Book Publishing Tax Credit.

This book was produced using FSC®-certified, acid-free paper, processed chlorine free and printed with soya-based inks.

Disclaimer

The actions described in this book may be considered inherently dangerous activities. Individuals undertake these activities at their own risk. The information put forth in this guide has been collected from a variety of sources and is not guaranteed to be completely accurate or reliable. Many conditions and some information may change owing to weather and numerous other factors beyond the control of the authors and publishers. Individual climbers and/or hikers must determine the risks, use their own judgment, and take full responsibility for their actions. Do not depend on any information found in this book for your own personal safety. Your safety depends on your own good judgment based on your skills, education, and experience.

   It is up to the users of this guidebook to acquire the necessary skills for safe experiences and to exercise caution in potentially hazardous areas. The authors and publishers of this guide accept no responsibility for your actions or the results that occur from another's actions, choices, or judgments. If you have any doubt as to your safety or your ability to attempt anything described in this guidebook, do not attempt it.

Contents

Introduction

The national and provincial mountain parks in British Columbia receive millions of visitors annually, but of these countless sightseers, only a very small fraction actually get out and explore the backcountry. What's more, the vast majority of the local population has never experienced the wonders that the mountain parks offer. It is my experience that the primary reason for not pursuing this beauty is that people lack the necessary knowledge and guidance. This guidebook is intended to encourage beginner and intermediate backpackers and scramblers to explore the backcountry amid the most beautiful scenery on the planet.

The book focuses on inspiring people to participate in these physically and mentally rewarding activities with minimal risk and effort. These wilderness sports that seem so daunting can become enjoyable passions when the appropriate guidance and encouragement are provided. Many of us aspire to hike, but do not know how. That is why I wrote this book.

Once the reader takes part in the adventures described here, they will discover an entirely new common bond with others, and they will encounter an entire world that only a few have been a part of. The effects of these accomplishments fortify the body and soul profoundly.

The book is divided into two activity categories: scrambling and backpacking. Assistance is presented for both groups in purchasing gear, including clothing, tents, cookware and stoves, sleeping bags and boots. Preparation and planning for all aspects of these backcountry journeys is explained as well. These pointers will completely prepare anyone with little or no experience to enter the hills and forests and explore the mountain parks.

Here you'll find the easiest backpacking and scrambling trips in the parks, including route information consisting of trailhead locations, GPS coordinates and visible landmarks. Trip time and distance, elevation changes, and of course summits and destinations, are marked as well.

There are many mountains in the parks system whose summits are easily accessible, and for anyone who visits the parks of British Columbia, just the sight of these peaks leaves one wanting to do more than merely gaze at them. The undeniable urge to actually get to the top is overwhelming. Not only does this guidebook encourage aspiring hikers to reach the top of these mountains, it will show them how to accomplish this seemingly impossible task with moderate ease.

I wrote this book for aspiring adventurers: to get them going into the backcountry and show them how to backpack into the most breathtaking regions in the world to experience the utter splendour of what has always been there waiting for them.

Tumbling/Ochre Junction Campground. We stopped long enough to realize that some campgrounds are too primitive. Since there wasn't even an outhouse, we decided to continue on to Tumbling Creek Campground.

Chapter 1
Backpacking Equipment

Purchasing backpacking equipment is an important investment, so you should take the time, effort and care to make quality decisions. The choices should not be as carefree as making a trip to a big-box store and buying the cheapest gear available. In fact, the standard rule is that the lighter the equipment is, the more expensive it turns out to be. Cost and quality become the difference between an efficient, lightweight, comfortable backpacking trip and a heavy, tedious, backbreaking, painful one.

Backpacks

When shopping for a backpack, speak with a qualified person in a reputable outfitting store and set aside considerable time for fitting. Each person is unique, and a proper fit is vital for successful trekking. Backpacks are categorized as either internal frame or external frame design.

Internal frame

The advantages of the internal frame style of backpack include its body-hugging capability and lower centre of gravity. Both of these characteristics result in superior balance, with freer arm movement and less bounce. The internal frame pack is also less likely to get hung up on tree branches and overhangs. The disadvantages are a bit of a trade-off, however, because although the lower centre of gravity creates better balance, it will put more stress on the shoulder harnesses, and the snugger body fit will generate perspiration on the wearer's back. An air mesh frame will help to counteract the effects of excessive sweat, though, as it permits air circulation between the pack and the backpacker's body. Because of this, the air circulation benefit now is no longer an exclusive feature of external frame backpacks.

External frame

The external frame backpack is less popular because of its awkward manoeuvrability. It does allow for larger loads, though, with the ability to lash objects onto the frame, making the pack easier to load and unload. It also lets air circulate between you and your pack, although this gap compromises balance. The external frame backpack has a higher centre of gravity, resulting in a more erect body posture.

Very seldom are external frame packs seen on the trail today, so the remainder of this discussion will involve only internal frame backpacks. Internal frame packs are loaded from either the top (top loaders) or the side (panel loaders). More advanced backpacks have the convenience of both top and side access.

Top loaders

This has now become the standard, most common type of backpack. The best argument for a top loader is the easy loading capability, as their basic design is a tube shape with a drawstring on top. This design is great for stuffing gear into, because the pack expands outward as gear is stuffed into it from the top. Additionally, the top loader has no zippers in critical pressure areas, so these packs can withstand excessive overloading, whereas the panel loader must be zipped up after it has been loaded.

Panel loaders

Panel loaders are outfitted with a huge, u-shaped, zippered opening on the back or side of the pack. The benefit of this design is easy access to articles near the bottom without having to unpack the entire load. The problems with this style are that panel loaders cannot be packed as densely as top loaders, and that the zipper is under constant pressure when the pack is fully loaded, and rupturing can occur.

Additional features

Other extras to look for in a backpack are simple items such as side pockets, external lash straps for securing bulky items to the outside, and compression straps to stabilize the load. A divider inside a backpack is an additional benefit, as it permits easier access inside and less stress on the base of the pack. A divider usually separates the lower third of the pack from the upper two-thirds, and limits the gravitational tendency for everything to pile up at the bottom.

Fitting a backpack

Torso length, not overall body height, is the measuring guide for fitting a pack. Fitting should be worked out in the standing position with the feet shoulder-width apart to allow the effect of gravity to give a more accurate reading. In this stance, measure the distance from the first thoracic vertebra (the prominent one where the neck meets the upper back) down to the sacral base (just below the bottom vertebra in the low back). This distance will provide the torso length. Shorter than 45 cm indicates a small pack, while 45 to 50 cm is considered a medium size. A torso longer than 50 cm takes a large backpack.

After determining the approximate size, throw the pack on your back. It should be stuffed with a few camping articles to add some weight and bulk, expanding the pack to its loaded size and providing more of a real-life simulation. The pack should be adjusted so that the weight is distributed to the hips and shoulders equally and so the hip belt rests below the waist at the hips. Make sure that the load-lift straps can be easily accessed by reaching behind your ears. A sternum strap is important, as it assists in determining the forward and backward centre of gravity, but its position on your sternum should also be decided by comfort. Most sternum straps can be raised or lowered to gain maximum comfort.

Clothing

The three fundamentals required for a successful trip are dryness, warmth and comfort. Although warmth and dryness go hand in hand, comfort is similarly important. With the ever-changing weather in mountain regions, these three crucial requirements are necessary to maintain a happy, enthused outing.

Undergarments and shirts

Given that the perspiration generated on a hike can create as much moisture in clothing as a heavy downpour, it is vital to purchase the appropriate clothing for both inevitabilities. Although cotton and wool may be comfortable, they have a tendency to absorb moisture and broadcast it throughout the rest of the garment. Consequently, when they get wet they will remain that way for some time. That is why a water-resistant, wickable fabric is preferable.

Wickable fabric is chemically treated 100 per cent non-cotton polyester, which is designed to expel moisture. It works on the principle of removing moisture from the skin and dispersing it into the atmosphere instead of absorbing it. It does the same with externally applied moisture. At least three different companies produce wickable material, but Patagonia's Capilene 3 is by far the best performer.

When it is near the end of the day and the sun is going down, the temperature can drop significantly within minutes and a wet cotton shirt can bring on chills and clamminess, greatly increasing the chances of hypothermia. Wickable material, however, can be dry by the time you get your tent set up, which makes for a more comfortable night.

To get the maximum benefit from wickable material, you should wear it in layers. The skin layer pushes moisture out to the external layer, and from there out into the atmosphere. Another wonderful feature of this fabric is that it is so tightly woven that it resists the sun and the bugs but still allows skin to breathe.

An alternative to wickable material is a polyester and nylon thread, as it will still repel rainwater better than cotton. An application of a water resistant chemical product such as Nikwax TX.Direct will create a resilient, wax-like coating on the material. This solution is mixed in the washing machine with the polyester shirt and run through a normal wash cycle. It is not waterproof, but it resists water quite well.

Outerwear

Over top of shirts, the next layer of material should be a jacket, preferably fleece. Fleece comes in a variety of thicknesses and qualities. Although this retains warmth and moderate amounts of dryness, it will trap moisture from the inside as it is repelled from the skin. Therefore, recognizing when to remove the fleece is important, as it should be a warming layer only and not used during a strenuous part of a hike. Fleece is warm, lightweight and reasonably compressible.

Another practical alternative for an outer layer is down-filled clothing. Although down is light, compressible and warm, once wet it becomes heavy, bulky and cold. Even if caught in a light summer shower it soon becomes a burden.

Pants

Absolutely never wear jeans as hiking pants. They are far too heavy and cumbersome; they absorb water; and the material is extremely thick, creating excessive amounts of perspiration. Jeans do not have an elastic waistband, and not even a belt will keep them up when wearing a backpack. As well, they cause chafing of the sensitive skin of the inner thigh and groin. When jeans get wet, they also become heavier and take days to dry out.

Synthetic material is the best choice for hiking, as polyester and nylon are much lighter and more compressible for packing than cotton. Synthetics are also warm and have the ability to repel water. Once more, wickable material is an excellent choice. During the heat of the day, when short pants can be worn, the same materials should be used, again avoiding cotton. Wearing shorts in a light shower keeps you cool, saves the hassle of donning rain pants and reduces the chances of getting your long pants wet, which may be needed later in the evening.

Raingear

Raingear is a critical component of any hike. Even on cloudless, hot days, a thunderhead could be lurking behind the next mountain. A light mountain drizzle can be quite nice, but a daylong downpour is not very pleasant. Being prepared for a cloudburst will make or break a successful summit. There are only two serious materials and two styles of raingear to consider. Let's look at the materials first.

Gore-Tex is the best rain material yet invented, but because it is the best, it is also the most expensive. Other manufacturers have tried to duplicate it, to no avail. Gore-Tex works on a similar principle as Capilene 3, as it pulls the moisture from underlying material and expels it as vapour through tiny pores in the fabric. The great advantage of this system is that only vapour can sneak out through these tiny pores, and for that same reason only vapour can sneak back in. Rain droplets cannot get through. Therefore, when your body temperature rises, the resultant heat converts the perspiration into vapour, which escapes through the Gore-Tex micropores and into the atmosphere, allowing underlying clothing to remain dry even in the rain.

The other material used in raingear is pure polyurethane backing with a 100 per cent nylon face. There are some variants, such as polyvinyl chloride (PVC) and polyester, but they all ultimately have the same properties. They perform exceptionally well to keep the water out, but they don't breathe from the inside outward. Perspiration gets trapped inside the jacket, creating a moist environment. To counteract this, some models come with zippered armpit and chest vents to compensate for the inadequate ventilation.

The greatest payoff for the polyurethane and nylon fabric is that it is about one-fifth the price of Gore-Tex.

These various materials are used in two styles of raingear: the poncho and the full pant and jacket. The poncho style should only be used for day hikes, when shelter is close by. The poncho is too ineffective, as well as awkward and bulky, making even simple hand operations or removing a pack rather tedious. The other glaring drawback is the gaping hole at the bottom, exposing the lower body to the elements. The lower limbs become wet from water splashing up from the ground and from runoff from the poncho itself, allowing precious body heat to be lost. Never depend on a poncho raincoat when scrambling. At high altitudes, the loss of heat combined with damp clothing could rapidly lead to extreme hypothermia.

The pant and jacket style retains heat very well, and if properly secured at the wrists and ankles, this design should keep you comfortably sealed from the elements. The jacket and pant style also allows much freer movement, keeps moisture out and retains body heat.

Gloves

Gloves are a piece of equipment that may seem unnecessary when packing on a glorious hot day, but even on a bright, blue-sky summer day, subzero temperatures are common on mountain summits. A mixture of wool, Lycra and spandex materials is very versatile, creating a fabric that is warm and elastic. Ideal for the outdoors, these gloves are lightweight and fold up into a little ball for packing. A waterproof treatment for these gloves is also available. Lightweight glove liners made of Thinsulate or comparable material are a viable alternative. Again, these are lightweight and compressible and can be stuffed anywhere in the pack.

Boots and socks

Comfort and support are particularly important when looking for the proper boot. Do not buy a large fit with the intent of wearing layers of socks for warmth, because retaining warmth is actually the responsibility of the footwear. A large-fitting boot will produce blisters and foot cramps and cannot be broken in properly. Conversely, a tight fit will impede blood flow and create cramping in your feet.

It is important to spend some time with a knowledgeable outfitter and get expert help with this crucial purchase. Tell your salesperson what the boot's primary function will be, the type of terrain you expect and the distances you plan to go. It is necessary as a backpacker and a scrambler to buy good-quality footwear. There are many different types of leather and synthetics to choose from, so it is vital that you sample footwear until you find the right pair for you. You do not want your boots to let you down in bad weather or rough terrain.

High-cut fabric or leather boots with an inner membrane of Gore-Tex or Sympatex offer good support and most importantly can be waterproofed. One-piece leather boots provide superior support and are the most waterproof, since they have fewer seams. They are very durable, and leather has natural moisture-wicking capabilities.

With either of these designs, a wickable inner lining such as Cambrelle is advisable to absorb perspiration and push it up and out through the leather or Gore-Tex membrane. Some boots are made with a leather lining for comfort, but the leather absorbs moisture and holds it longer than Cambrelle, making the inside of the boot wet and mushy.

Most boots will require additional waterproofing. This should be done long before the first hike, permitting ample time for the product to be absorbed into the boot. Either the spray-on petroleum type or the rub-in type will help to keep your feet warm and dry.

Proper socks are also important, and there are several combinations to choose from, including a mixture of acrylic, wool, nylon, spandex or polypropylene, worsted wool and stretch nylon. Some manufacturers use cotton mixed with Hollofil. The decision depends on two main factors: an individual's level of perspiration and their tolerance of synthetic materials. If you have significant tolerance for synthetic material, then a wickable material is recommended to keep moisture away from feet. Alternatively, try wool socks, as they are somewhat wickable. Never use cotton socks, however, as they readily absorb moisture. When cotton socks get wet, they slide around inside your boots, creating hot spots on your heels and the balls of your feet.

Another suggestion is to use wickable liners inside your socks. These draw the moisture out from your feet and into the sock almost immediately, keeping the feet free of perspiration moisture.

Sleeping bags

Sleeping bags are categorized by fill, shell, size, shape, internal space, weight, compatibility and temperature rating.

The required temperature rating depends on the time of year the bag will be used, the elevation and the local climate and environment. Be aware that weather in the Rockies can change overnight, and it is not uncommon to encounter temperatures below freezing combined with snow even in July and August. Therefore, you should consider a bag that is suitable for subzero temperatures even if you only intend to use it in the summer.

Of the several types of fill, down is the best choice. The rest are all synthetic imitations of down. The superb features of down are that it has high loft (the higher the loft, the warmer you will be), it is lightweight and has great compressibility. The only drawback is that when down gets wet it becomes useless. It will no longer keep you warm, it loses its loft and gets heavy and it takes forever to dry. You might as well pull up your tent and head home.

The synthetics are an adequate, less costly alternative to down, and of course, some are better than others. The main advantage of synthetics over down is that when they get wet, they will dry out in a reasonable time, allowing the journey to continue. Synthetics do not have the loft or compressibility that down has, though, and they are slightly heavier. Hollofil, Hollofil 2 and Quallofil, though considered a technological alternative to down, are the least-regarded synthetic fills. These bags are bulky, heavy and do not compress well, but they are inexpensive. Primaloft, Primaloft 2, Liteloft, Microloft and Thermolite Extreme are better performers but still they are not the best. Although they are quite compressible, they will not stand up very well in the long run.

Polarguard, Polarguard 3D and Polarguard HV are the top synthetic fills and currently hold 75 per cent of the market. They are very compressible, have good loft, which they maintain longer than the others, and they are very durable. They are also lighter than the other synthetic fills.

When purchasing a sleeping bag, choose it for size as well. There are mainly three adult sizes: small, medium and large. The bag should leave room to pull the hood around your head while leaving a few inches at the bottom for leg movement, but not too much legroom. All empty space in the bag must be warmed with body heat, and wasted space means wasted heat. Spending the night warming up dead space in the bottom of a sleeping bag can make for a very long, cold night. Consequently, when it comes to retaining warmth, a mummy bag is far superior to a rectangular bag. A common problem with some campers, however, is that they feel claustrophobic in a mummy bag, so if you have difficulty in elevators, you will probably have trouble in a mummy bag. To respond to this problem, some mummy bags are outfitted with elastic waist and leg bands to allow for expansion.

Another relevant feature is a double-ended zipper (having a zipper pull at both the top and the bottom of the bag), as this allows partial unzipping along the bottom to permit cooling and movement. There are good rectangular bags available for those who just cannot tolerate a mummy bag.

Sleeping pads

The purpose of a sleeping pad is to supply comfort and insulation from the cold ground. Without one of these, the smooth, soft ground will soon feel like cold, hard concrete.

Of the three types of sleeping pads, the self-inflating kind is preferable, as it offers greater cushioned comfort and good insulation. They are light, compact and easily compressed to fit into a backpack. A minor downside with self-inflating pads is that they can puncture, but they are easily repaired and are usually equipped with a repair kit. Self-inflating pads come in either a full body length size or a three-quarter body length model for less weight and bulk. These single-chambered, self-inflating air mattresses become one-half to three-quarters of an inch thick when fully blown up. The term self-inflator is used because the mattress will inflate of its own accord when unpacked and rolled out with the valves open. Some lung work is still required to attain maximum loft. A more recent addition to the self-inflation family is the down-filled mat. These dramatically reduce heat loss and compress smaller, as most down products do, but they are a nuisance to inflate. Down becomes lumpy and ineffective when moist, so the pad must be inflated with a bellows. The down mat design consists of ribbed chambers with baffles to prevent the clumping of down, as well as allowing a higher loft. The design and materials provide superior comfort and warmth, but at a price four to five times that of a standard self-inflator. A variation on this product is the non-down, ribbed self-inflator. This chambered, baffled mattress supplies loft and comfort without the warmth of down, while still giving greater warmth than the standard models.

The other main category of sleeping pads is the closed-cell type, which does not cushion as well as the self-inflating pads but offers better insulation for a comparable thickness. These are somewhat bulky, though, and do not compress at all, so they must be rolled up and strapped to the outside of the pack. The only advantage of closed-cell pads is that they are far less expensive than the self-inflating ones.

Lastly, "blue foam" pads are very cheap, but are often of little use. To sleep comfortably on the ground, you need a sleeping pad with enough loft to keep you comfortable and warm. Blue foam is just not dense enough or thick enough.

Tents

The two most important factors to consider when purchasing a tent are weight and quality. The remaining features such as ventilation, materials, quality of manufacture and ease of setup will fall into place correspondingly. Choosing a tent is really quite uncomplicated, but a tent should nevertheless be purchased at a backpacking retailer rather than a department store. Department stores and warehouse depots generally do not carry the quality of tent required for backpacking.

The style of tent, whether dome or tunnel, is an individual taste, as is the size. Style and size ultimately determine the weight, so decide whether the tent is going to be used by a single hiker or a group. Once you've decided on size, the choice of style is fairly easy. A dome tent suits a group of three or more, while the tunnel type is generally for a single hiker or a pair.

Poles are a key component of the tent. Aluminum and tempered aluminum poles are superior to fibreglass, as they are stronger, more flexible and lighter. They are, of course, more expensive. Even so, the choice is usually made for you, as the higher-end tents will come equipped with aluminum, shock-corded poles.

The material of the tent is also a consideration. A three-season tent, made of lightweight nylon, is sufficient for late spring, summer and early fall backpacking and is the most common type. For camping in winter, a mountaineering tent, four-season tent or even a convertible tent is advisable. These are made of nylon and polyester, making them heavier.

Speed and ease of setting up a tent are especially important in the dark or in adverse weather. There are three basic designs for attaching a tent to its poles: clip style, pole sleeves or the grommet system, though the simple grommet system is rarely used anymore. Colour-coded clips with matching-colour pole ends are possibly the easiest method for pitching a tent.

Proper ventilation is another concern when looking at tents. On a hot summer night with a barrage of insects, ventilation becomes essential. Double doors with no-see-um mesh are a bonus, as cool air is allowed to flow without opening a flap and letting the bugs in. Some models also have a mesh ceiling to inspire stargazing.

Even if the manufacturer insists their tent is waterproof, it still needs to be seam-sealed. This is a straightforward procedure requiring little effort but a bit of time. Set up the tent in an open area such as a backyard, and roll or brush the sealant on every stitch, seam and zipper. Do the same to the fly tarp. Use a seam sealer that is recommended by the tent manufacturer.

A footprint is a tent accessory that is particularly valuable and is simply a second floor that goes under the bottom of the tent. Footprints are not a standard component; they are add-ons that are usually hard to find and quite costly. It is far easier and cheaper to purchase thin nylon from a fabric outlet and have it sewn by a local tailor. The footprint should be slightly larger than the floor of the tent, with grommets installed where the tent pole ends are situated. A footprint increases the longevity of your tent floor material as well as keeping it dry.

Cookware

It seems that with any backpacking equipment, there is always a tradeoff between weight and quality, and cookware is no exception. With four types of material to choose from, the decision becomes a personal preference. Aluminum, stainless steel, non-stick coated aluminum and titanium are the common choices.

Heat dispersion on the bottom of the pot depends on the thickness and type of metal. Thicker is definitely better for heat distribution, but of course it is heavier to carry. Aluminum has one-third the density of stainless steel, so when using aluminum the result will be a thicker pot with less weight. Aluminum is also a better conductor of heat than stainless steel is, even if the stainless steel is thicker.

So why even consider stainless steel? Stainless steel is stronger and does not dent or scorch nearly as easily as aluminum. Accordingly, stainless will last longer and is easier to clean than aluminum.

The third material, titanium, is incredibly light, extremely strong and effortless to clean. The downside is its susceptibility to scorching: if the meal is not constantly stirred, the bottom of the pot will burn and so will dinner. Titanium is also incredibly expensive.

Non-stick aluminum is the best all-round choice. Its density is comparable to the relative thickness of steel, and therefore the heat is dispersed evenly. It is stronger than basic aluminum cookware and it is by far the easiest to clean. However, non-stick coated aluminum is two to three times the cost of the stainless steel and is somewhat heavier.

Backcountry stoves

There are two types of backcountry stoves to choose from: those that use canister fuel and those that use liquid fuel.

The canister type comes in a variety of styles, and all of them use pressurized fuel that is either butane or a mixture of butane and propane. Of the two kinds of canister fuels, the blended-fuel type produces a hotter flame. Even so, all fuel canisters will fade in cold weather and at high altitudes.

Almost all liquid-fuel stove systems use inexpensive white gas, which burns more efficiently than either type of canister fuel. The liquid fuel stove is also more efficient at high altitudes and cold temperatures. What's more, when a liquid fuel stove runs out of gas, it only requires refilling the empty cylinder, whereas with canister fuel the entire canister has to be replaced.

The canister stove may burn somewhat more powerfully than the liquid fuel stove at first, but it loses its efficiency proportionately as pressure and fuel decrease. What's more, with most brands of canister units, there is no effective way of controlling the fuel output. Liquid gas stoves, on the other hand, come equipped with a pump and a flow control valve, allowing far greater regulation of the fuel. The Mountain Safety Research (MSR) "Pocket Rocket," however, is an extremely lightweight, ready-to-use canister system that does permit control of fuel flow.

The only real benefit of the pressurized canister system is its easy set-up and use. You just attach the canister, light the stove, and it heats up immediately, while the liquid gas stoves are more finicky and time-consuming to set up. But even among liquid gas stoves, there are levels of craftsmanship, and MSR's WhisperLite Internationale has been proven reliable for decades. It boils water quickly and simmers very effectively, even in high winds, rain and cold and at high altitudes.

MSR WhisperLite Internationale

MSR Pocket Rocket

Water containers

The types of water containers are different for backpacking and scrambling, but with either activity, attaching the canister to the outside of the pack is preferable for easy access. For backpacking, a single 1-litre container is adequate, as you'll frequently find streams and lakes along the trail. At least two 1-litre containers should be carried while scrambling, though, since water is not readily available there.

In fact, on a scramble, when you come upon clean water, it is good practice to rehydrate yourself immediately and replenish your bottles, because there usually is no water on the sides of mountains or their summits. It is a common error to rely on what may be shown on a map or on remembering that there was water up this mountain last year. Always take advantage of any water you come across, without depending on what may lie ahead, as more often than not there will not be any water whatsoever on a mountain scramble. Go with the intent of taking with you all the water you'll need.

Conversely, a backpacking route will almost always have plenty of water along its course, and if not, the campgrounds are always situated near a clean water source. Hydration is imperative to avoid muscle cramping, light-headedness, fainting and heatstroke.

Presently, there is so much rapidly changing controversy about carcinogens in bottle linings that if I recommend something now, it will probably be outdated already. I will leave this decision to you.

Additional equipment

Items that are necessary for a successful backpack trip but do not require detailed descriptions are items such as:

bug spray	flashlight	all-purpose tool
bear spray	matches	toilet paper
sunscreen	water filter system	toque
extra clips and straps	hiking pole(s)	bandana
short length of rope		

Hoary marmot. This little guy seemed to be hypnotized by the mist rising out of this beautiful valley. This was a gorgeous, crisp fall morning.

Chapter 2
Backcountry Management

Most beginner backpackers do not know what to expect at a campground after a day of hiking, and this can be somewhat unnerving. Without the knowledge of where to camp, cook, store food, get water, urinate, dispose of waste or brush your teeth, a backcountry blunder is inevitable. This sort of difficulty may not be important to some campers, but the backcountry campground requires a community effort if it is to remain pristine, and many hikers take this on as a passion.

Campsite location

Selecting a campsite is relatively easy in the Canadian Rockies backcountry. The campgrounds in the national parks are designated areas, and random camping is rarely permitted. Sites are easily located in the campgrounds: some are marked, some have tables, some even have wood shavings to set your tent on, but all of them are at least trampled down.

The first consideration in deciding on a campsite is proximity to water. Almost all campgrounds are located along streams or lakes, but the decision partly depends on the weather. A good general rule is to stay 50 to 75 m away from water on cooler days, since the temperature may be as much as 10 degrees cooler beside the water. On hot days, camping a little closer to water is preferable. Naturally, the water should also be conveniently accessible for repeatedly refilling your water containers.

Level ground is also of primary importance. Sleeping on well-graded, flat earth is not always possible at campgrounds, but the more level the ground is, the more peaceful your night will be. Even with no-slip sleeping pads there is still a tendency to skid down the pad if camped on a slope. If there is no choice, and there is only sloped ground available, be certain to sleep with your head higher than your feet to avoid awakening with a pounding headache.

Explore the region for insect life as well. Anthills, beehives and stagnant water (mosquitoes) should be passed by. Insect-infested trees not only present the obvious insect problem, but the affected tree may be structurally weakened as well. Additionally, look for rodent dens, game trails, and porcupines in trees.

Ideally, your campsite will have trees to shelter your tent from the wind. But you should examine these surrounding trees for potential danger. Campsites with dead or diseased trees or branches, as well as trees that have fallen and are leaning on others, should be avoided. A stand of trees is one of the safest places to be during a lightning storm, but camping under a single tall tree is dangerous because lightning will go for the single tallest object in an area.

If the campground's dining area is communal, do not set up too close to it. Not all campers clean up after themselves, and animals quite often do this for them. Since some campsites are equipped with rustic picnic tables, you may find yourself cooking and eating close to your tent, so be absolutely sure that no scraps have been left behind.

Proximity to the outhouse is also a consideration. Although there are typically not any tent sites next to outhouses, some are closer than others. There is no nightlight to switch on, and stumbling through the dark, bumping into tents and trees, is painful and embarrassing. Campers that urinate beside their tents are endangering all other backpackers in the campground because the odour attracts bears and rodents.

Tent set-up

After selecting a tent pad, the next step is to erect the tent. The tent should be set up soon after arrival, as the weather can change quickly and darkness can arrive sooner than anticipated. It may be tempting to have a drink or lunch first, but the tent should go up before too long, leaving the exploring and playing until later. The tent will be your only shelter from the elements for a few days, and if it is not ready before an unexpected cloudburst arrives, then sleeping bags, clothes and equipment become drenched and the trip is ruined.

If your camp is somewhat organized before you leave for some day hiking, then you can at least get warm and dry if the good weather does not hold. After the tent is up, the sleeping pads, bags and clothing should be tossed inside immediately – again, to keep them dry in the event of rain. Next, the food, cooking utensils and all other odorous belongings should be pulled up the bear poles. Backpacks, now empty of food, should be placed under the tent vestibule. Bears and rodents are enticed by almost any smell, so when your food is placed up the bear pole, your soap, bug spray, sunscreen, toothpaste, stove, pots and anything else that emits any scent should all go up with it.

Consider setting up your tent with the door facing south so the morning sun can shine in to warm you up. Wind direction should be noted if the bugs are bad or if it is a hot evening. Tents with twin doors should be oriented so as to allow the breeze to circulate through.

Cooking/eating area

In the backcountry, where you eat is just as important as what you eat. Some campgrounds have common areas where everyone cooks and eats, while others have a table at each campsite. Communal areas are intended to keep food and odours away from tents, and they should be used when provided. These areas are usually central and well marked with signage or a designated structure. If they are not marked, search for obvious signs of use, like rocks or logs in a circle or signs of cooking. Cook and eat at these areas until the meal is finished so that food is not spread throughout the campground.

Estimating the quantity of food to cook is tricky but essential, as there are no garburators or wastecans, and all of the food cooked must be consumed. Food waste cannot be tossed into the outhouse, because this attracts rodents, and it certainly cannot be thrown into the streams or lakes. All campgrounds have a designated grey-water disposal area, but it is intended for wastewater that may contain only a few scraps, not for throwing out leftovers. The only other alternative is to contain the waste in a plastic bag or container and consume it later or pack it out. After eating, all morsels of food, paper, matches and plastic must be picked up from the ground or table. Every last scrap.

Food should not be consumed near the tent, and eating in the tent is absolutely discouraged, including gum and candy. Bears are attracted to the scent of food, and if anything has been chewed in the tent, a bear's nose will lead him there. Never cook in your tent: not only will the food odours be absorbed into the tent fabric but you'd also be at risk of carbon monoxide poisoning.

Washing your dishes

Cleaning up utensils, dishes and pots in the backcountry is a bit of an art and an attempt should be made to use as little water and soap as possible. Heating water in the cooking pot you've just used not only detaches stuck food but also provides hot water for cleaning the other items. A bit of biodegradable liquid camp soap on a reusable cloth works well to remove particles from dishes and utensils. The soap, water and waste should be dumped into the grey-water site. Rinse with a bit of clean water and wipe dry.

Washing yourself

Hygiene in the woods is necessary but not difficult. Before cooking any meal or making a hot beverage, use some of the boiled water to wash with. Do not wait until after the meal when the pot is grimy or after you have done the dishes and must boil more water, as this only wastes valuable fuel. Pour the hot water onto a clean cloth and apply a dab of camp soap, then wash body parts with this soaped cloth. Pour hot water onto another clean cloth and use for rinsing. Wring these cloths out into the grey water area and hang them to dry.

Brushing teeth is just as easy, and you can get odourless toothpaste with organic ingredients at most health food stores. A small amount of water with a modest amount of toothpaste is all you need. Brush and then spit again into the grey water pit. Please do not wash your body or brush your teeth in the lakes or streams. If everyone uses one small, designated grey-water area, then waste and pollution are not spread all over the countryside.

A small bottle of antibacterial gel also comes in handy.

Outhouses

We all know what should be done in there, but some of us tend to overuse this convenient facility. The only waste that goes in, other than the obvious, is toilet paper. No food, garbage, cans or plastic should be thrown down this hole. These items must be used or packed out. Skunks and porcupines are attracted to such smells and can really ruin a campground's atmosphere.

Maintaining the campground

The minimalist rule for campground maintenance is to try to leave your campsite in better shape than you found it. Stay on the established trails leading to the water source, bear poles and outhouse. Trampling on delicate flora can eradicate them quickly, as these plants only have a short time to grow and reproduce. If they are destroyed during this short window, they cannot reproduce the following year. The same principle applies to digging drainage trenches, uprooting rocks, picking flowers and snapping branches off trees. The campground should be left as close to its natural state as possible.

Stanley Peak viewed from Mount Whymper.
Even in mid-summer resilient snow lingers
in the rocky shadows.

Chapter 3
Scrambling

I would like to emphasize that the scrambles in this book are not necessarily easy, but they are the easiest I have accomplished in all my years and thousands of kilometres of trekking. Scrambling is a lot of work and there really aren't any easy scrambles. They all travel directly upward and very rarely provide any respite.

Fitness

To climb mountains and venture into the backcountry, strong legs and strong lungs are equally important. Many factors determine the level of fitness an individual will need to accomplish the goals set out in this guide. Even though one does not require an athlete's physique, it is still important to tone up muscles and work heart and lungs long before the season arrives. You cannot decide in June that it is time to get in shape for a scramble in July and expect to enjoy it. It just will not work. We all agree that everyone is unique, so each and every one of us will have distinctive expectations. Our discipline will not be the same either. But you get out what you put in, and it is much easier to scramble up a mountain while being in trim condition with strong heart and lungs than being flabby and gasping for air. Every kilo of weight you lose in the winter and spring is a kilo less you'll have to haul up a mountain or into the bush. Every extra kilometre logged on a treadmill will be rewarded with less effort in the summer.

The three basic components to mountain physical fitness are muscle strength, muscle flexibility and cardiovascular strength. There are numerous ways to increase your heart health and exercise your lungs. Walking, swimming and cycling are great. Stair climbers, jogging and low-impact aerobics are also superb ways to gain wind and endurance. If you live in a snowy climate, snowshoeing and cross-country skiing are activities that will improve circulation and strengthen your legs. The best method to prepare yourself for the scrambling season is to walk up mountains or hills that may be in your area.

Muscle strength and flexibility are just as significant as the cardiovascular system, and there are just as many ways to work on this. All of the previously mentioned activities will boost leg power, but they will not improve the suppleness of these muscles. Basic stretching exercises can be found on the Internet or in libraries, but for something a bit more intense, try yoga.

For the most part, everyone will work at their own pace and with the equipment at their disposal. It should be rather simple to enter into a plan for the off-season, but try a bit of variety to ease the boredom. If it becomes increasingly difficult to develop a fitness program, consult a professional. Discuss your goals and comfort level and get started.

Scrambling equipment

Scrambling equipment is essentially the same as backpacking equipment, with only a few changes. The pack and footwear will be different, and some notable additions must be highlighted.

Daypack

The features to look for in a scrambling pack are similar to those of a full backpack, but the pack is smaller. The main difference between the two activities is that scrambling is more physically intense and therefore creates excessive perspiration. A moderate backpack trip may take three to five hours, whereas an easy scramble will take five to eight hours. A scramble of 1000 m of elevation gain is, of course, only 1 km in distance, but for the most part, it is uphill and will take the better part of a day. That same distance while backpacking should take no longer than 10 to 20 minutes. With these key elements to consider, weight, air mesh frame, and padding become vital.

The area of most perspiration will be the region of most contact between the pack and your back. Perspiration cannot escape if there is a plain nylon pack frame resting on the spine. An air mesh frame will absorb moisture and even repel it in some cases. Ideally, an elevated mesh, which outlines contact areas, not only absorbs moisture but also reduces the amount of friction between pack frame and body.

Additionally, with the tremendous physical work of scrambling, it becomes apparent that you should pack as little weight as you can possibly get away with. Purchasing a smaller pack in itself reduces weight, but it also forces you to cut down on the extra, non-essential gear. Daypack sizes vary greatly, but a scrambling pack should be in the range of 20 to 35 litres capacity.

Hip belts and shoulder straps that are padded and adjustable are optional features that should be considered. They enable far greater comfort, permitting transference of the pack weight from shoulders to hips and vice versa. A sternum strap is another necessary item, as it pulls the load forward when cinched, easing the natural tendency of the pack to pull the load backward. These small features may not seem important now, but it is a tremendous relief during an all-day climb when your load can be rearranged ever so slightly.

A lid that allows you to shift and elevate the top load is another feature that makes for a less strenuous hike, because it transfers the weight and the centre of gravity. A proper lid can carry frequently used items like bug spray and sunscreen.

Ideally, the scrambler's daypack should have external straps for fastening items that require immediate access such as an ice axe or helmet.

Footwear

Although hiking boots are suitable for scrambling, a lighter "approach" shoe is recommended. These shoes are especially suited for scree slopes and rockhopping. Due to their lighter weight, there is generally less fatigue on the legs, feet and ankles. Approach shoes are generally constructed of synthetic materials, so there is the risk of getting wet feet. Good approach shoes will have a ring of rubber around the entire shoe, including the toe, flanks and heels, as these areas are susceptible to damage from scraping on rocks while climbing. Good grip is essential, more for descending than ascending, and a cushioned insole is also advisable. As with good hiking boots, a backpacking outfitter will have the best selection and quality. Try on several pairs until you find the right one for you.

Additional equipment

Many items that are necessary for a successful backpack trip are also essential for a scramble. A few other items recommended for a scramble are:

bug spray	matches	flashlight
bear spray	bandana	toilet paper
sunscreen	hiking pole	helmet
extra clips and straps	water filter system	emergency foil blanket
short length of rope	toque	all-purpose tool
ice axe (only required for high elevations)		

The Kicking Horse River, CPR rail line, and the Trans-Canada Highway viewed from the Mount Field summit.

Chapter 4
First Aid

A first aid kit should contain everything necessary to treat anything from mosquito bites to fractured legs to gaping wounds. As frightening as it may seem, if an accident occurs there will be no help. Even if you have cell phone service, assistance is still hours away. It is therefore essential to be prepared to care for yourselves. Many backcountry first aid kits not only hold all of the essential tools but also come with instructions for treating emergency injuries. Take a kit along on all trips.

Since blisters and hypothermia are the most prevalent ailments suffered while trekking, they will be the only ones discussed here.

Blisters can occur on all areas of the feet, including ankles. The best way to treat a blister is to avoid getting one at all, and knowing how blisters occur will help prevent them. Blistering results from friction, and friction between material (socks and boots) and your skin creates a shearing stress on the skin. This shearing action causes separation of the supple outer layer of skin that covers the deeper, more secure layers. As the bones in your foot move one way and the boot moves another, the skin is trapped between the two and rubs on the sock material, creating a hot spot. Due to this constantly repeating friction, the outer layer of skin at this spot becomes separated from the tougher inner layers, and the area of the separation gradually fills with lymphatic fluid, creating a blister. Treating a blister before it becomes a full-blown mess is imperative.

At the first sign of a potential blister, stop walking and attend to the problem immediately. Many great trips have been ruined by deciding to limp the last kilometre or two to the campground. Treating a hot spot is easy, but before administering any treatment, wash and dry the afflicted area first. Then apply an antibiotic ointment and cover the spot with moleskin or Spenco 2nd Skin. For a fully developed blister, the treatment is only slightly different. Again, clean and dry the affected section before proceeding with the treatment, as infection can easily occur if the area is not kept clean. After this, the bubble must be broken with a needle to release the fluid. Disinfect the needle with an antiseptic wipe, puncture the blister and release as much of the fluid as possible by applying pressure with clean hands. After the screaming subsides, spread an antibiotic ointment over the blister and cover with moleskin or Spenco 2nd Skin. This should be repeated two or three times a day in the same manner, washing and drying the area anew and applying fresh ointment and moleskin.

Hypothermia is another common syndrome easily acquired but easily avoided, and being prepared is the best prevention. Even on the clearest, sunniest day in the mountains, the weather will change without notice. While standing at the base of a mountain on a hot day it is hard to believe that the temperature at the summit can be below freezing, but quite often this is the case. Dress accordingly for the heat, but make certain you've packed cold-weather apparel too. Gloves, toques, jackets and an emergency blanket are indispensable articles to take when either backpacking or scrambling.

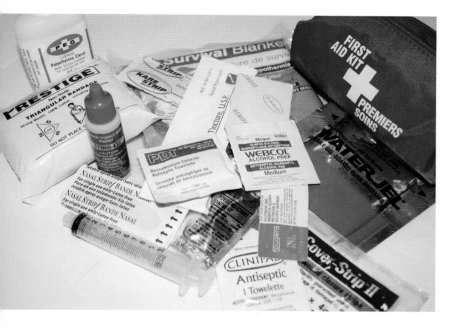

Emerald Lake. One of many pleasures of backpacking to Yoho Lake is this lakeside stroll along the entire western shore of Emerald Lake.

Chapter 5
Backpacking Trips

1. BOSTOCK PASS CAMPGROUND

The Bostock Pass Campground is not really a dedicated campground. Random camping is permitted in the meadows, but you must adhere to Parks Canada's guidelines. In random camping areas, campsites must be at least 50 m from trails, 70 m from water bodies and 5 km from trailheads. Additionally, Parks Canada would like campers to search for previously laid down vegetation to pitch their tents. The route consists of a gradual climb through a deep-green forest, eventually opening up to a spectacular meadow with astounding views of nearby mountains.

DIFFICULTY ▲ ▲ ▲
DISTANCE: 9 KM
ELEVATION GAIN: 722 M

Trailhead: GPS: N51 13 48.2 W117 40 10.2
                                            Elevation: 1032 m

Bostock Pass Campground: GPS: N51 16 35.8 W117 43 11.9
                                            Elevation: 1754 m

Trailhead: Take the Trans-Canada Highway to 19.5 km west from the Rogers Pass Centre and 50.5 km east of the town of Revelstoke, BC. The parking area is on the north side of the highway and well marked.

The path begins by crossing to the east side of Bostock Creek just as you're leaving the parking lot. It then enters a humid, dark-green Interior rainforest of Engelmann spruce and western hemlock with ferns, mosses and lupines. An uphill climb of switchbacks begins as you enter the forest and continues until the creek is a substantial distance below. The trail continues to climb along a steep, treed hillside with little room to

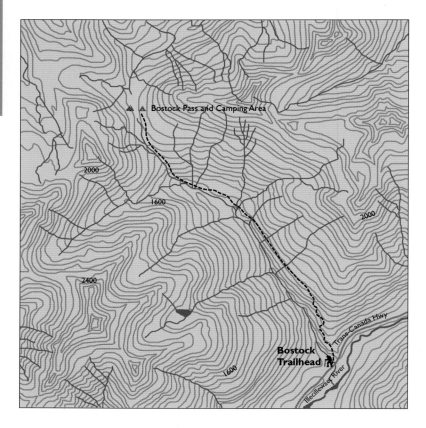

manoeuvre. If you look carefully to the left (west) you may see the hut of the Christiana snow research station perched on Christiana Ridge on the easterly rise of Mount Fidelity.

The trail and the hillside regain an even keel as they enter a clearing where the path crosses a small stream feeding into Bostock Creek. Throughout the journey, several creek crossings traverse Bostock Creek's countless large and smaller feeders. Some crossings have bridges, some have logs and some are jumpers. You will have to make your own way on a few of these crossings, as some are littered with fallen trees and rubble.

Gradually, the trail ascends through small clearings containing thigh-deep brush that can and will scrape up your legs if you are not properly clothed. Hiking shorts are not recommended. On a cloudless day, the clearings and crossings can reveal abundant views of neighbouring peaks, with Mount Fidelity, Corbin Peak and Mount McGill figuring prominently among them.

The forest begins the characteristic thinning of a trail approaching the subalpine zone. As the route continues its upward winding journey, the transition to subalpine is subtle yet noticeable. Continue the upward trek, and in due course the path emerges from subalpine forest to the expanse of the upper meadow at Bostock Pass.

This unique meadow is dotted with islands of trees because it lies in the subalpine and not completely above the treeline. Still, the trees are not thick enough or clumped close enough together to constrain your view of the surrounding mountaintops.

Bostock history

In 1896, Caribou Creek, pass and valley were renamed in honour of British-born Canadian Senator Hewitt Bostock. At one time, an abundance of mountain caribou populated this pass, but since their numbers had significantly dwindled by then, the original name seemed inappropriate, and the uncommon practice of renaming encountered no opposition. Bostock's careers were varied and abundant, as he excelled at logging, printing, politics, mining, real estate, fruit farming and ranching.

Hewitt Bostock was born in Walton Heath, Surrey, on May 31, 1864. He attended Trinity College in Cambridge from 1882 to 1885, earning a degree in mathematics. After obtaining his Masters in 1890, he was called to the bar in 1888, but he never practised law. Bostock's first visit to Canada was in 1886 to see Ottawa and the Parliament buildings, but it was during a later excursion while touring North America, China and Japan, that he visited the Kamloops, BC, region, where he purchased a ranch, as a retreat, at present-day Monte Creek in 1888. In 1893, he and his wife, Lizzie, moved to Victoria, BC, and visited the ranch only periodically for holidays.

The next few years were fast paced and quite busy for Bostock. Around 1893 or '94, he started the Kootenay Lumber Company, establishing the prosperous sawmill town called Comaplix, on the northeast arm of Upper

Arrow Lake at the mouth of the Incomappleux River. He established a weekly newspaper, *The Province*, in Victoria in 1894. Four years later, under pressure from business associates, he moved his presses to Vancouver and established a daily, also called *The Province*, which still exists today.

Bostock's political career began when he and his family established roots back in Monte Creek in 1894. The 1896 federal election saw Bostock run successfully for the Liberals in Yale–Cariboo. He was appointed to the Senate in 1904. In 1914 he became the Liberal party leader in the upper house, and in 1921 he was named speaker of the Senate.

During the span between 1898 and 1900, Bostock constructed at least two business blocks on the main street of Kamloops and became president of the Tranquille Creek Hydraulic & Quartz Mining Co. Ltd.

This extremely busy man died of uremia in 1930. He was buried on the property in Monte Creek alongside the small church he built in 1926, which still stands today. The church is visible from the Monte Creek interchange on the northeast side of the Hwy. 97 on-ramp to the Trans-Canada Highway. Mount Hewitt Bostock is in the Cascade Range, just 20 km northeast of the village of Boston Bar, BC, in what formerly was the Yale–Cariboo riding where he was first elected MP in 1896.

Bostock Pass "campground" in early May. Although it was a beautiful spring day, this summit was blanketed with snow. In the mountains, always be prepared for the unexpected.

The author and Peter Peller stop for a break on the way to the Bostock Pass summit.

2. COPPERSTAIN PASS CAMPGROUND

There is nothing quite like this pass. You will experience over 1200 hectares (3,000 acres) of rolling meadows that undulate through the expanse of a long, wide, shallow valley. This is quite possibly the largest wild meadow you will ever come across. Oh, and take your wallet, because there's beer. Purcell Mountain Lodge is ideally situated within this vast meadow, and, at least on our last trip, they served beer to hikers.

DIFFICULTY ⛰ ⛰ ⛰ ⛰ ⛰
DISTANCE: 16 KM
ELEVATION GAIN: 1213 M

Trailhead:	GPS: N51 21 43.8 W117 25 47.9
	Elevation: 875 m
Copperstain Pass Campground:	GPS: N51 17 19.8 W117 18 33.8
	Elevation: 2088 m

Trailhead: Some 11 km east of the Rogers Pass Centre, watch for a large hiking sign directing you to a minor side road on the east flank of the Trans-Canada Highway. The highway sign is marked "Beaver Valley." The pavement ends, giving way to gravel almost immediately, and begins a wide-sweeping right-hand turn that soon completes 180°. In just less than 1 km, you'll cross a narrow, single-lane bridge, and about 250 m later meet a fork in the road. Take the left fork, and within another 300 m the large gravel parking lot reveals itself. An outhouse is conveniently located on your right.

The trail begins as a short uphill hike into a forest of thick-based Douglas fir and western cedar spread out between much thinner stands of Engelmann spruce. For the first 4.8 km, the route consists of mild inclines followed by level, park-like stretches, always staying close to the Beaver River. For the first hour, what you hear more often than the river, though, is the sound of the highway. The path is wide and flat, and at sections it becomes interchangeable with a vacated fire road.

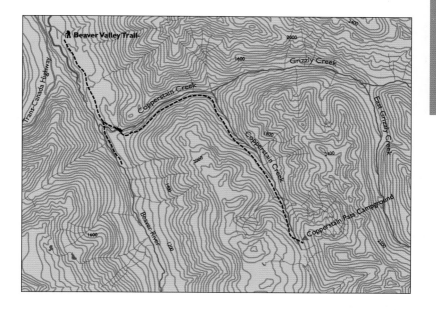

I have never seen more bear signs in any stretch of hiking than in the first 4.8 km of this route. Fresh scat, root diggings, turned-over rocks, claw scrapings on trees – all were abundant. The proprietor at the Purcell Mountain Lodge informed us that a grizzly mother and her cub had recently been seen frequenting the meadows. The truth of this claim was obvious from the massive diggings throughout the field.

At 4.8 km the journey reaches a junction that divides the route into two distinct directions. Taking the south (right) fork takes you into the wilderness of the Beaver River Valley, while staying east (left) carries on to your destination. As the trail splits, the sound of the Beaver River gives way to the sounds of the forest. So far, there has been only a mild elevation gain of 152 m.

At the 6-km mark, a right-hand fork leads to an old structure, the Grizzly Cabin, which appears to still be functional. On our last trip here, however, the place was padlocked. We had heard mention of a campground here as well, but we could not find it. The main path stays on the left branch. About 250 m farther on, you cross Grizzly Creek on a suspension bridge. After exploring a small meadow for 10 to 15 minutes, the trail goes back into the forest and begins to climb. Views are limited as you rise from valley to alpine. There are a few breaks in the trees as you cross streams and gullies, but mostly it is an uphill hike on a forest track with frequent switchbacks.

After an hour to an hour and a half of this, the landscape begins to unfold as mountains over to your left become evident. Copperstain Creek trickles in its valley below, also to your left. Continue upward for another 30 to 45 minutes. On the left again, a burn of trees is unmistakable, and Copperstain Mountain is directly ahead to the south as you approach Copperstain Creek Pass.

When you arrive at the pass, brace yourself for unimaginable sights. At the far western (right) edge, this massive field unassumingly drops straight down some 1200 m to the bottom of the Beaver River Valley. Across the valley the peaks of Mount Sir Donald, Terminal Peak, Uto Peak and many others reach for the sky. Straight ahead sits Copperstain Mountain and a limitless vision of grass and flowers. It is just such an incredible experience. Simply breathtaking. Enjoy the 2.5-km stroll to the campground nestled in trees on the left slope of the valley. Wooden-plank tent pads are propped to support tents above the moist ground. Ensure you bring sleeping pads, as the wood floor can be quite uncomfortable.

Day hikes are plentiful here. I will leave that up to you. The lodge is not visible from the campsite; it is about 1 km up the valley, high up on the western plateau of the pass.

Copperstain Pass and Beaver Valley history

During his 1882 exploration to discover a pass through the Selkirk Mountains, Major Albert Bowman Rogers chose the route from the east through the Beaver River Valley. Since he was the first white man to visit this pristine valley, he had the privilege of naming the river. Due to the numerous beaver that inhabited the valley, the name for the river became clear. The Beaver Valley and the surrounding area, though, were not named until eight years later, by Harold Topham.

Topham was a novice mountaineer from Britain who arrived at Glacier House in 1890 with aspirations of making some first ascents in the untouched Selkirk Mountains. He was one among many who had the same desires, and by July he was hiking, climbing and exploring with his friend Henry Forster and Swiss amateur mountaineer Emil Huber. The threesome explored most of the Asulkan region, with highlights such as mounts Purity and Sugarloaf, Glacier Circle and Black Glacier. During these explorations, Topham and Huber marked this stream in their journal as the Beaver River, helping to consolidate Rogers's original name. The valley henceforth became known as the Beaver Valley.

The river was called Beaver Creek on Rev. W.S. Green's 1888 map of the valley, and somewhat later it appeared as Beavermouth Creek on an 1892 map of the "Rocky and Selkirk Mountains." However, on July 24, 1904, the Department of the Interior's topographical map of the Selkirk Range relied on A.O. Wheeler's 1902 report "The Selkirk Range," with the map being published in 1906.

3. EVA LAKE CAMPGROUND

This 26 km of winding pavement, climbing 1455 m to the trailhead, is quite an impressive drive. In fact, I have heard many road explorers call it the most beautiful scenery they have ever seen in their lives. But as pretty as this drive is, though, it becomes trifling for those who venture beyond the parking lot when they get there. This hike is magnificent, and I cannot understand why people would drive this road and not explore the trail. It is a wonderful opportunity to easily experience outstanding mountain habitat.

DIFFICULTY ▲ ▲
DISTANCE: 6 KM
ELEVATION GAIN: 25 M

Trailhead:	GPS: N51 02 48.9 W118 08 32.2
	Elevation: 1925 m
Eva Lake Campground:	GPS: N51 04 51.7 W118 06 38.3
	Elevation: 1950 m

Trailhead: The Meadows in the Sky Parkway is found just outside of the eastern edge of the township of Revelstoke, BC. Follow the signage to the Mount Revelstoke National Park kiosk, pay the fee and proceed upward on the parkway. The trailhead is beyond the parking lot, and there is a free shuttle bus that takes tourists up the final 2 km of pavement (or you can walk). The trailhead is at the northeast end of the bus turnaround.

The path begins a slight decline almost immediately, and the spectacular benefits of beginning a hike so far up begin to pay off just as quickly, as the views begin right away.

The temporary descent ends within 500 m, where the forest becomes thinner. An interpretive sign reminds travellers that they are in bear country and presents logical tips for avoiding encounters. An open hillside of low brush and wildflowers is the first in a succession of pockets of beautiful rolling meadows lasting for about a kilometre.

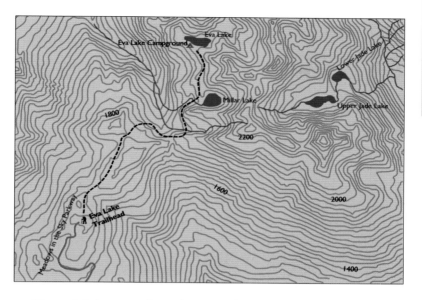

The path brings you through varying landscapes for the next 2 km as it passes through more meadows, crosses a stream, rises onto a boardwalk, heads back into a forest of Engelmann spruce and opens up to a series of wide, steep rockslide slopes. The openness of the rockslide slopes yields absolutely amazing panoramas of the Selkirk Mountains to the north, with the Monashees dominating the west. Peaks of note to the northeast are mounts Dickey and Coursier, nearly 7 km distant. This is a rare trek that grants such diverse, substantial gifts with such minimal effort. Do not take it for granted.

About an hour into the hike, with 4.8 km behind you, you'll see a remnant of the imperial system of measurement in the form of a three-mile marker. Soon after, the previously flat, easy trail reminds you that you are in the mountains by presenting a short, five-minute burst of switchbacks. Signage at the summit of the switchbacks shows a branching of the route, to the right to Jade Lakes and left to Eva Lake. Fork and sign are at the 5.6-km mark, so only a quick 400-m stroll remains.

The level track to Eva Lake proceeds leftward, quickly crossing a wide open avalanche hill that reveals vistas of the Monashee Range. You then duck back into the forest, climbing slightly, just before reaching the lake and the campground. In the midst of this tranquil setting is an historic log cabin.

Eva Lake history

Eva Lake was discovered by Eva Hobbs in 1910 during a three-week camping trip to Balsam Lake with her two sisters and two other women. Hobbs had joined the newly formed Revelstoke Mountaineering Club the previous year, and during the women's stay at Balsam Lake, five gentlemen from the club arrived to build a cabin at the lake. In exchange for a day's labour and a cooked meal, the women asked the men to take a day to go exploring with them. As this large party crested a ridge, Hobbs was in the lead and was first to spot the undiscovered lake that would bear her name.

Hobbs was a schoolteacher in Revelstoke and became an avid hiker at the urging of the school principal, A.E. Miller, for whom nearby Miller Lake is named. Miller would have four or five of his teachers join his explorations into the Mount Revelstoke area, and many would climb to the summit with him long before a trail was cut. One of his first companions on those hikes was C.R. Macdonald, the local druggist, for whom Macdonald's Bluff, on Mount Revelstoke, is named.

Construction of the route to the summit of Mount Revelstoke was completed in 1908, by the hard work and perseverance of local residents. The network of trails to the various lakes would take many more years to finish, as the exploration of this mountain was quite gradual compared to the rapid growth of mountaineering in nearby Glacier National Park. Citizens lobbied provincial and federal governments to get Mount Revelstoke declared a national park, and in 1914 their efforts succeeded. During the push for a park, the locals also convinced the governments to pave the route they had broken to the summit. The Meadows in the Sky Parkway took 16 years to finish, becoming complete in 1927. The reason for the name of the parkway is evident, with an abundance of wildflowers in the alpine region of the mountain. This truly is a wondrous place to hike.

An abundance of streams contribute to the astounding
beauty displayed on the hike to Eva and Jade lakes.

Eva Lake. Mount Revelstoke National Park.

53

4. JADE LAKES CAMPGROUND

A beautiful, windy, uphill drive of 26 km brings you to the brink of the trail-head. Scenic as it is, though, the drive does not match the natural beauty that the hike in to Jade Lakes has to offer. This is a relatively level walk until you reach the fork to Eva Lake. From this intersection, the trail climbs steadily up the southern slope of Mount Williamson to an elevation of 2162 m before dropping to 1819 m at the Upper Jade Lake campsite. A remarkable journey.

DIFFICULTY ▲ ▲
DISTANCE: 9 KM
ELEVATION GAIN: 343 M FROM JADE PASS SUMMIT TO UPPER JADE LAKE

Trailhead:	GPS: N51 02 48.9 W118 08 32.2
	Elevation: 1925 m
Jade Pass Summit:	GPS: N51 04 18.8 W118 05 13.3
	Elevation: 2162 m
Upper Jade Lake Campground:	GPS: N51 04 11.0 W118 04 34.0
	Elevation: 1819 m

Trailhead: On the east edge of the outskirts of Revelstoke, BC, the Meadows in the Sky Parkway exits the Trans-Canada Highway and begins its upward journey toward the wondrous Mount Revelstoke backcountry. Stop at the kiosk at the entrance to the Skyway to pay your fee, and then drive ever upward, winding around switchbacks on a smooth, paved road. Park in the spacious lot and make your way to the trailhead either on foot or by free shuttle bus. Look across the pavement to the northeast to find the marked trailhead.

The journey begins with a brief, slow drop in altitude right away and continues for about 500 m. Remember that you have driven 26 km and reached the summit of Mount Revelstoke, so the vistas up here are already enormous.

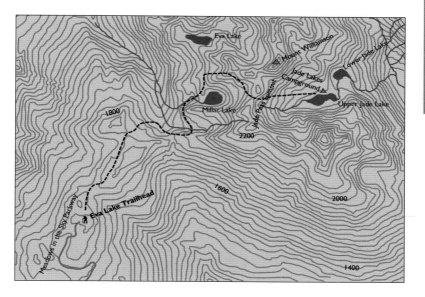

As the forest thins and the trail levels, an interpretive sign reminds travellers that they are in bear country and presents logical tips for avoiding encounters. An open hillside of low brush and wildflowers is the first in a succession of pockets of beautiful rolling meadows lasting for about a kilometre.

The journey takes you through several meadows, crosses a stream, rises onto a boardwalk, heads back into a forest of Engelmann spruce and then opens up to a series of wide, steep rockslide slopes over the next 2 km. The views afforded by the exposed rockslides are absolutely amazing panoramas of the Selkirks to the north and the Monashees to the west. Looking northeast, mounts Coursier and Dickey are among many amazing sights as you wander through the upper subalpine. The hike is so effortless, and presents such diversity, that a small hint of guilt seems to linger.

Although these trails are in a Canadian national park, they still have remnants of the imperial system of measurement. Just after the first hour of hiking, for example, you'll come upon a three-mile marker. With 4.8 km behind you, the previously flat, easy hike soon reminds you that you are in the mountains, with a short, five-minute burst of switchbacks. Signage at the

The Monashee Range seen on the western horizon
from the Jade Lakes trail.

The trail to Eva and Jade lakes teems with avalanche
slopes that provide incredible panoramas.

summit of the switchbacks marks a branching of the route, to the right to Jade Lakes and left to Eva Lake. The fork and sign are at the 5.6-km mark.

From this fork, the path takes off uphill and wraps around the south slope of Mount Williamson. Trekking toward Jade Lakes has been easy so far, but now the trail starts to climb for the next 20 minutes, passing Miller Lake on its way to Jade Pass, eventually reaching 2162 m at the summit. The clear, blue-green waters of Miller Lake are only a small part of the attractions on the wide open path to the summit, where endless strings of peaks line the horizon. Before dashing down to the campground, take a break at the summit and enjoy what you have worked for. The snow-capped Inverness Peaks stand 4 km to the northeast at a true bearing of 240°. Three kilometres due north, the Clachnacudainn Range is easier to see than pronounce.

With the trail dropping an incredible 343 m from the pass, the way down to Upper Jade Lake is quite evident. Only a few tent pads are available, and they are accompanied by a bear pole and an outhouse.

The Rockwall

The next six routes are all part of a system commonly known as The Rockwall. This guide takes each campground as a separate individual trek, outlining each one's distance, elevation and landmarks from the point of origin that will require the shortest distance to get to the campground. Consequently, there is some repetition, as a few of these routes have the same trailhead, and travel the same path for a distance, until branching off on their own.

By inspecting the maps, it is plain to see that these campsites are situated in a pattern that encourages looping and multi-day treks. As this guide is designed to be used to encourage single-day, beginner expeditions, details of looping treks are not established, but distances are posted to help readers make informed decisions before embarking on multi-day hikes. Be aware that elevation and trail condition details are not given for routes beyond terminal campgrounds.

HELMET FALLS CAMPGROUND TO TUMBLING CREEK CAMPGROUND: 11.6 KM
TUMBLING CREEK CAMPGROUND TO NUMA CREEK CAMPGROUND: 7.9 KM
NUMA CREEK CAMPGROUND TO FLOE LAKE CAMPGROUND: 9.5 KM

5. FLOE LAKE CAMPGROUND

Without question, Floe Lake is one of the most stunning spots on the planet. This is a hike that should not be neglected, though it is a lot of work. Some things in life are important enough to work very hard for, though, and I would never send you on a journey that didn't merit its difficulty.

The devastating forest fire season of 2003 left much of northern Kootenay National Park inaccessible, with some parts completely closed to public hiking. Fortunately, on July 16, 2005, the Floe Lake Trail was reopened. Although fallen burnt timber has been cleared, it is a good idea to follow Parks Canada's recommendations for travelling in a post-forest-fire forest:

> *Don't go in windy conditions, especially with rainfall or snow.*
> *Travel quickly to reduce exposure time.*
> *Stop only in open, flat areas, keeping at least the distance of a tree's height between you and the nearest tree.*

Nonetheless, the trek through the burn adds a unique appeal to an already distinct hike. Pack light, as the last 2.5 km is a 300- to 400-m climb without a level break. Floe Lake is the beginning of one end of the "Rockwall Trail," which extends for more than 40 km beneath the east edge of The Rockwall. The Rockwall itself is a ridge of Ottertail limestone several hundred metres high and 31 km long, culminating to the north at Mount Drysdale.

DIFFICULTY ▲ ▲ ▲ ▲ ▲
DISTANCE: 10.5 KM
ELEVATION GAIN: 723 M

Trailhead: GPS: N51 04 38.8 W116 02 56.4
                              Elevation: 1351 m

Floe Lake Campground: GPS: N51 03 08.3 W116 08 06.4
                              Elevation: 2022 m

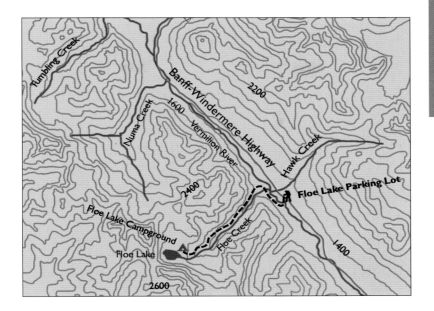

Trailhead: From the Castle Junction interchange, proceed south onto Hwy. 93. The parking area is located 32 km south of the Castle Mountain Junction on the west (right-hand) side of the highway.

The hike starts off as a flat walk through a forest of charred pine and spruce. The open, flat path soon descends slightly to the Vermilion River, and within 500 m the trail crosses the river over a newly constructed bridge. The path levels off after a brief climb out of the river valley only to descend again 15 minutes later to cross Floe Creek. From this crossing, the balance of the trip follows the right side of the Floe Creek drainage channel up to Floe Lake, though most of the route runs several hundred metres above the creek.

One of my favourite features of Kootenay Park, setting it aside from other regions of the Rockies, is the wide, steep avalanche slopes that seem to appear without notice. Allowing spectacular scenery even in dense forest, these slopes suddenly open to present stunning unexpected views across valleys and mountainsides. Such slopes are numerous throughout this spectacular trek.

Five minutes after exiting the Floe Creek crossing, the familiar feeling of a gradual climb transforming into switchbacks becomes evident and eventually develops into the dominant theme. Twenty minutes later the trail levels off and Floe Creek is so distant below to your left that you barely hear it anymore.

The hike continues through the severely fire-damaged forest of spruce and lodgepole pine. It is astonishing to witness this natural devastation, but even more astonishing to observe the forest regenerating itself. Saplings are beginning to grow, and much of the undergrowth and grasses have returned in an unstoppable resolve to flourish. This is a marvellous, unique experience. Do not hesitate to stop and look; this all a part of your journey.

Over the next hour and a quarter, the trek is rather uneventful as it rambles through the forest, interrupted by great slopes, stream crossings and some minor rises until reaching the 8-km mark. It is at this spot that the trail takes a steep uphill turn, zigzagging precipitously upward to gain 300 to 400 m within 2.5 km. As these gruelling switchbacks begin, mature forest resumes and the viewing becomes limited, though there are a few spots along the way that allow you to look back across the valley. But you are going to be too tired and sore anyway to even turn around and look. So, head to the ground and keep trudging. At times like this, I find that solving math problems in my head distracts me from the obvious toil. I suggest you too try something to occupy your mind.

Just as you reach the summit of this climb, thoroughly exhausted, the magnificent Rockwall comes into full view. Stop for a moment to catch your breath and focus on the goal. The campground is only another 500 m farther, and the hike graciously levels off ten minutes before you reach the lake.

Indeed, Floe Lake is another treasure offered to us by the Rocky Mountains, being surrounded by meadow, mountain, forest and ice. The far shore of the lake is enclosed by cliffs and glaciers, while the sides are lined with subalpine fir and small alpine meadows. The lake's name comes from small icebergs that calve into the lake from the glacier that feeds it at the far end. Just the sight of such dazzling beauty renders the steep climb of moments past nothing less than petty.

Spring meltwater gently rolls into Floe Lake.

The still waters of Floe Lake reflect beautifully, even on a cloudy day.

61

6. HELMET FALLS CAMPGROUND

If not for the overall distance, the journey to these wondrous falls would be reasonably effortless. As Kootenay National Park does not possess the notoriety of the neighbouring Banff and Yoho parks, it is often less travelled. So it is not too surprising to come across such a gem as this without any fanfare or very much human traffic. The place is remarkably unknown and amazingly easily accessed. Helmet Falls has a total height of 352 m that spills over two tiers. The single drop forms from two streams which join at mid-fall. The two streams originate from two separate glaciers in the massive Washmawapta Icefield.

DIFFICULTY ▲ ▲ ▲ ▲
DISTANCE: 15 KM
ELEVATION GAIN: 319 M

Trailhead:	GPS: N51 10 12.3 W116 08 50.1
	Elevation: 1443 m
Helmet Falls Campground:	GPS: N51 11 46.6 W116 18 17.8
	Elevation: 1762 m

Trailhead: From Castle Junction, drive south on the Banff–Windermere Highway (Hwy. 93) for 19.6 km to the Paint Pots parking lot, on the west side of the highway. The trailhead is well marked, at the edge of the forest on the west side of the parking lot.

The route leaves the parking lot quite uneventfully. A straight, level path even accommodates wheelchair access within the first minute, diverting to the left of the main route. Both paths descend gently, converging shortly before crossing the Vermilion River by way of a short suspension bridge. On the other side of the river, the astounding 360° panoramas include peaks of the Vermilion Range dominating the west and northwest horizon while the Ball Range towers against the eastern sky. If you can tear yourself away from this engrossing encounter, follow the track along

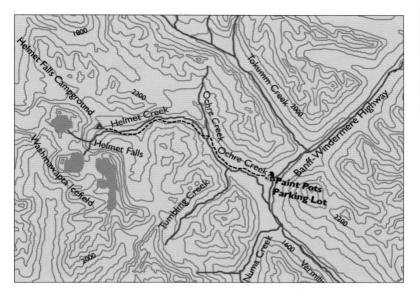

the stream and into the forest to arrive at the lower Paint Pots. This should take no longer than ten minutes.

The Paint Pots are a rare find and should be explored, at least for a few minutes. The trail through this mud-lover's paradise is distinct and well worn. Sections that are excessively dirty are overlaid with wooden planks. The muddy path inclines slightly to gain the upper section of the Paint Pots, where the water in the lower flats originates. At the top of the ochre beds, the path becomes indiscernible and you will be left standing at the top of the beds, wondering where to go. If you look straight over the small mud flat up here, you will see that the path picks up again at the far end of the outlet of the main bed. The track is visible as it enters the forest beside an aged marker. Either walk across the mud (it is really quite firm and shallow) or follow a faint path to your right that circumnavigates the small mud flat and ochre pond.

The trail into the forest narrows where an old, rough-looking sign guides you to Helmet/Ochre Creek, Tumbling Creek and Helmet Falls campgrounds. A stairway of railway ties assists your entrance into the woods. Within another five minutes, a sign steers you to stay straight on the path and you'll feel a mild elevation gain. A couple of small streams are crossed as the journey through forest of spruce and pine levels off. At about the 3.5-km mark, you'll cross a magnificent avalanche slope of shrubs, wild berries and flowers.

After crossing the slope, the route pierces the forest for another six to eight minutes, coming across signs in a small, cleared intersection 3.9 km from the trailhead. Helmet Creek Falls Campground is another 11.1 km straight up the main path. As the hike departs the junction it begins a slight uphill climb and the forest becomes sparser with thicker trees. Two kilometres from the intersection, the route opens up to a small field of red paintbrushes, yellow and purple daisies and a variety of grasses. There are great views of north and west peaks from this engaging little field.

The next ten minutes of the hike takes the trail down to the river bottom, where tributaries joining Ochre Creek make for some minor rock-hopping. Helmet/Ochre Creek Campground is situated on the far bank of Ochre Creek. From here, 8.8 km remain to Helmet Creek Campground. Stroll through the campground as the route continues along the eastern shoreline of Helmet Creek and crosses it over a sturdy bridge. The path leaves the riverbank to climb a series of switchbacks for about 500 m. For the next 3 km, up here, the journey continues through avalanche slopes and a rolling forest with views of Helmet Creek far below. Eventually you drop down to the river again, skirting it for about 2 km and crossing it over another suspension bridge.

Leaving the river and entering the forest brings a welcome silence for a short time. Within the next 1.5 km the first glimpse of Helmet Falls will grab your attention. This site really caught us by surprise during our first hike to the campground. It is still far away from here, but is incredibly spectacular. The falls are 352 m high, seem to fall forever and are back-dropped by a massive limestone wall. Amazing. The trek finishes on a fairly level circuit of trees and meadow and finally descends over a bridge into the campground, after passing a Parks Canada warden cabin.

Helmet Falls. Kootenay National Park. The falls are
easily spotted as you approach the campground.

One of many well-maintained suspension bridges
throughout the Kootenay National Park backcountry
trail system.

65

7. HELMET/OCHRE JUNCTION CAMPGROUND

This is a flat, easy trip with a negligible change in elevation that travels through a pine and spruce forest filled with wonderful streams. A key highlight of the journey is the trip through the Paint Pots. Natives used the ochre from these beds for ceremonies, body painting and trade. Europeans first began exporting ochre in the early 1860s shortly after James Hector discovered the beds in 1858. The mineral had such commercial importance as pigment for paints that by the early 1900s ochre mining had started. The initial mining method was to hand-dig the ochre and carry it away by horse and wagon, but by the 1920s rail cars and horse-drawn scoops were implemented. Eventually, though, mining was phased out by the Parks system, and the last scoop was dredged in the early 1920s.

DIFFICULTY ▲ ▲ ▲
DISTANCE: 6.5 KM
ELEVATION GAIN: 62 M

Trailhead: GPS: N51 10 12.3 W116 08 50.1
Elevation: 1443 m

Helmet/Ochre Junction Campground: GPS: N51 11 34.2 W116 12 47.4
Elevation: 1505 m

Trailhead: The route leaves the parking lot uneventfully. A straight, level path accommodates wheelchair access within the first minute. Both trails descend gently to the Vermilion River to cross a short suspension bridge. At this position, the 360° panoramas are astounding. Peaks of the Vermilion Range dominate the west and northwest horizon, while the Ball Range towers in the eastern sky. If you can stop looking around long enough, follow the track along the stream and into the forest to arrive at the lower Paint Pots. This should take no longer than ten minutes.

The muddy path inclines slightly to gain the upper aspect of the Paint Pots. At the top of the ochre beds, the path becomes indiscernible, but it does pick up again at the far end after crossing the outlet of one of the

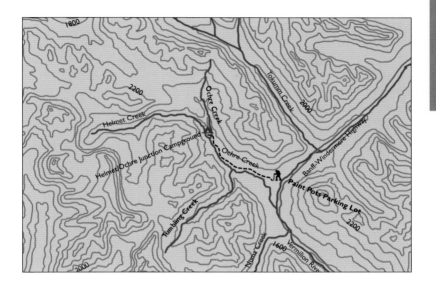

cones. The cones are formed from the iron oxide buildup at the outlet of cold mineral springs. They rise in height from the constant deposit of minerals at the base of the cone.

The trail into the forest narrows where an old, rough-looking sign guides you to Helmet/Ochre Creek, Tumbling Creek and Helmet Falls campgrounds. A stairway of railway ties assists your entrance into the woods. Within another five minutes, a sign steers you to stay straight on the path and you feel a mild elevation gain. Cross a couple of small streams and the trail through spruce and pine forest levels out.

At about the 3.5-km mark, you'll see a magnificent avalanche slope of shrubs, wild flowers and grasses. We saw a bear. Of the thousands – yes, thousands – of kilometres I have trekked, I have only had one single bear encounter. Actually, this was, um, barely an encounter at all. More of a happenstance. And the bear wasn't even aware we were having an encounter. We had my golden retriever, Summer, along and were about to walk out onto the above-mentioned grassy slope, but we'd stopped, as we usually do before entering such slopes, to check for bears. And sure enough, this time there was one, on the slope to the uphill side of the trail. It was too busy eating berries to realize we were there, or maybe was aware of us but just didn't care. We backed into the forest, returned to the trailhead and called it a day.

The lesson learned was to keep your dog on a leash when walking the backcountry trails. I know definitively that if Summer hadn't been leashed, she would have been exploring at least 50 m ahead of us. She would have trotted right onto that slope, torn after the bear, and then hightailed it back toward us with the bear in hot pursuit. So although restraining your dog in the wilderness may seem like a ridiculous rule, it is an essential one. Oh, and pick up your dog's poo, too.

After you've crossed this slope, it re-enters the forest for another six to eight minutes before reaching an intersection in a small clearing. This signed junction marks the 3.9-km mark of the hike. The Helmet/Ochre Junction campground is another 2.6 km straight up the main route. As the trail departs the junction it begins to climb slightly and the forest becomes sparser with thicker trees. Two kilometres from the intersection, the path opens up to a small field of red paintbrushes, yellow and purple daisies and a variety of grasses. There are great views of peaks to the north and west from the engaging little field.

The last ten minutes of the hike take the path down to the river, where tributaries joining Ochre Creek make for some minor rockhopping. The campground is situated on a premier spot if you enjoy the continual sound of rushing whitewater.

Vermilion River crossing en route to the Paint Pots and the Rockwall backcountry.

Upper Paint Pots outlet source.

Iron oxide cone formation at the Upper Paint Pots.
The cones are formed from the iron oxide buildup at
the outlet of cold mineral springs. They rise in height
from the constant deposit of minerals at the rim of
the cone.

69

8. TUMBLING/OCHRE JUNCTION CAMPGROUND

With an overall distance of 4.3 km and only 12 m of elevation gain, this is a pretty easy hike. This trip should be reserved for a late afternoon arrival into the Rockies. You know, one of those Fridays when you get off work a bit early, drive to the mountains and want to spend the night somewhere in a forest. This hike will take about an hour to arrive at the campground.

DIFFICULTY ▲
DISTANCE: 4.3 KM
ELEVATION GAIN: 12 M

Trailhead: GPS: N51 10 12.3 W116 08 50.1
                                             Elevation: 1443 m

Tumbling/Ochre Junction Campground: GPS: N51 10 37.8 W116 11 37.1
                                             Elevation: 1455 m

Trailhead: The route leaves from the Paint Pots parking lot, located 19.6 km south from the intersection of the Banff–Windermere Highway (Hwy. 93) and the Trans-Canada Highway at Castle Junction. The parking lot is directly off the west side of the highway, and the trailhead is at the west side of the lot.

The trail immediately enters the forest. As soon as the trek begins, the route splits, becoming wheelchair accessible down the left fork, a unique quality for any backcountry route. The two branches rejoin shortly after, just in time to cross the Vermilion River over a short suspension bridge. The bridge and the banks on both sides provide spectacular sights in all directions. On the eastern horizon is the Ball Range, while the west and northwest skies give you the Vermilion Range. Continue the path to the lower Paint Pots.

The muddy path carves through wide open lower flats of the Paint Pots for a few minutes and then inclines slightly to gain the upper area of the Paint Pots and ochre beds. The track fades here and you can either

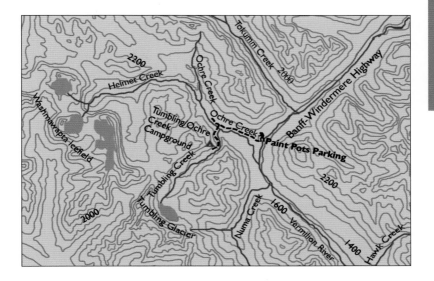

make your way around the muck and moisture by detouring to the right or simply barge directly across the small mudflat. Either way, it is a short inconvenience before reaching the sign that picks up the trail again. Before you cross, though, stop and check out the springs exiting the ground beneath your feet. There is so much iron oxide in these cold mineral springs that it forms cone-shaped structures that rise in height from the constant deposit of minerals at the base of the cone.

The entrance back onto the trail and into the forest is assisted by an old, tattered sign marking the way to Helmet/Ochre Creek, Tumbling Creek and Helmet Falls campgrounds. Walk up a stairway of recycled railway ties, and within five minutes you will come across another sign. As it suggests, stay straight on the path. The path now climbs slightly, crossing a couple of minor feeder streams before levelling again. You then come to a splendid, wide, long avalanche slope of shrubs and flowers, at the 3.5-km mark of the trek.

Head back into the pine and spruce forest at the far edge of the slope, but before you do this, stop and look around. Have a gaze up the hillside and down toward the creek below. Try to imagine the force of rushing, crashing snow that could mow down a forest, removing all evidence of sturdy trees, leaving brush, shrubs and flowers to flourish in their stead. Now, back into the forest, you will encounter a small intersection within six to eight minutes. There are a few signs and directions here, so pay close attention to ensure you take the correct path. Turn left at the junction and follow this path for 400 m. Cross Ochre Creek on a suspension bridge to a very primitive campground on the riverbank. Tent pads dot the shoreline and there's a privy along a trail into the forest. The place does not appear to have any bear poles.

Tumbling Creek. Kootenay National Park.

9. TUMBLING CREEK CAMPGROUND

The Tumbling Creek Campground hike provides an astounding menu of raging creeks, sweeping slopes that spill from mountaintops, vast open expanses, waterfalls and forest. This 11-km stretch of wilderness provides gorgeous views and incredible sounds. Tumbling Creek itself possesses a uniquely mesmerizing, captivating quality that seems to make the day slip by without notice. Enjoy its contagious indolence.

DIFFICULTY ▲ ▲ ▲ ▲
DISTANCE: 11 KM
ELEVATION GAIN: 445 M

Trailhead:	GPS: N51 10 12.3 W116 08 50.1
	Elevation: 1443 m
Tumbling Creek Campground:	GPS: N51 08 22.6 W116 14 08.7
	Elevation: 1888 m

Trailhead: Follow the Banff–Windermere Highway (Hwy. 93) 19.6 km south from Castle Junction to the Paint Pots parking lot on the west side of the highway. The trailhead is on the west side of the parking lot.

The route leaves the parking lot into a beautiful forest of Engelmann spruce and lodgepole pine. The path is well trodden and usually well populated for the first ten minutes, as this route to the Paint Pots is quite popular with roadside trekkers. Throughout your journeys, you will discover the same theme: many roadside attractions are littered with tourists who will look at you with bewilderment as you walk past them in full backpacking gear. They have no idea of what you are doing, where you could possibly be going or why you would do it.

A straight, level path affords wheelchair access within the first minute. Both routes descend gently to the Vermilion River to cross a short suspension bridge. At this position, the 360° panoramas are astounding. Peaks of the Vermilion Range dominate the west and northwest horizon,

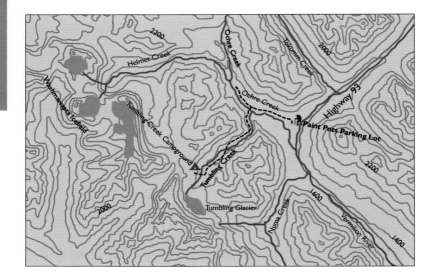

while the Ball Range towers over the span of the eastern sky. If you can stop looking around long enough, follow the trail along the stream and into the forest to arrive at the lower Paint Pots. This should take no longer than ten minutes.

The muddy path inclines slightly to gain the upper aspect of the Paint Pots. At the top of the ochre beds, the path becomes indiscernible, but it does pick up at the far end, after crossing the outlet of one of the cones. The cones are formed from the iron oxide buildup at the outlet of cold mineral springs. They rise in height from the deposit of minerals at the rim of the cone.

The trail into the forest narrows where an old, rough-looking sign guides you to Helmet/Ochre Creek, Tumbling Creek and Helmet Falls campgrounds. A stairway of railway ties assists the entrance into the woods. Within another five minutes, a sign steers you to stay straight on the path and you feel a mild elevation gain. After crossing a couple of small streams, the hike through spruce and pine forest levels off. At about the 3.5-km mark, you come to a magnificent avalanche slope of shrubs, flowers and maybe bears.

After crossing the slope, you re-enter the forest for another six to eight minutes and eventually come across signs in a small cleared intersection. Turn left to follow the trail another 7.1 km to Tumbling Creek Campground. Six to eight minutes later, the route crosses a suspension bridge, meets the Tumbling/Ochre Junction campground and passes through it quickly. Tumbling Creek sticks to your left flank for a few more minutes until the hike begins to switchback uphill. Ten minutes later the route levels off into a forest of spruce and pine.

The forest takes on an odd characteristic here as it begins to thin out, leaving only the thickest, strongest trees standing. Looking upward through the trees, it becomes apparent that the thinning results from years of bombardment from snow and debris sliding down the mountainside. Here, you can see the forest for the trees.

The forest continues to thin and will meet with an expected wide avalanche slope that periodically glances into forest. The journey progresses toward the campground in the midst of trees, shrubs, rocks and soil, meandering up and down through this paradise, and at 6.5 to 7 km into the journey, you cross Tumbling Creek over a short metal bridge. The reason for the name of the creek becomes evident the further upstream you go. This is not a deep, wide, raging river, but a creek that actually falls – tumbles – onto itself. It is steep enough and contains enough rock and debris that it truly does tumble rapidly down the valley.

Continue briefly uphill, to be rewarded with uncluttered views of the green, open slopes on both sides of the creek. Drainage down the slopes into Tumbling Creek is spectacular. An added bonus is the sight of Grey Mountain directly down the trail to the southwest. A couple of waterfalls in Tumbling Creek simply add to a magnificent day. Combine this with a bit of elevation gain within the forest and some stretches of creekside rambling and the day will soon be complete at Tumbling Creek Campground.

Tumbling Creek's namesake becomes evident as you hike along its banks. The tumbling roar is constantly with you.

Avalanche slopes are abundant in Kootenay National Park. The open slopes provide vistas not usually seen in other Rocky Mountain parks.

10. NUMA CREEK CAMPGROUND

This hike begins with a spectacular waterfall just off the parking lot. Because of this, the outing begins with an abundance of tourists posing in front of, and snapping photos of, this remarkable roadside attraction. With such an abundance of wondrous beauty filling this park, it is marvellous that so much of it is so easily accessible. Beyond Numa Falls, the bridge and the cameras, the picture becomes filled with forest, grassy slopes, flowers and streams. The destination is an accumulation of a wealth of streams. Some bridgeless creek crossing is required and flows can be dangerously high during runoff, so please be careful.

DIFFICULTY ▲ ▲ ▲
DISTANCE: 6.6 KM
ELEVATION GAIN: 139 M

Trailhead:	GPS: N51 07 58.4 W116 07 57.3
	Elevation: 1398 m
Numa Creek Campground:	GPS: N51 06 37.0 W116 10 59.6
	Elevation: 1537 m

Trailhead: Some 24 km south of Castle Junction, the Numa Falls roadside picnic area is easily located on the west side of the Banff–Windermere Highway (Hwy. 93). Parking is plentiful. Find the trail at the south end of the lot or follow the sound of the falls.

The expedition begins at the parking lot with a bridge crossing over the Vermilion River and the spectacular Numa Falls. The bridge appears to be reinforced to handle parking lot adventure seekers, as it is made of thick, solid steel. Weave your way through the tourists to burst onto the path and immediately turn left. Switchbacks begin almost right away, lasting for about 10 to 15 minutes before levelling off.

A kilometre of mindless stroll through a forest filled with Engelmann spruce is broken with a small high bridge over a dry gulch. A short-lived climb turns into a level crossing through an overgrown avalanche slope

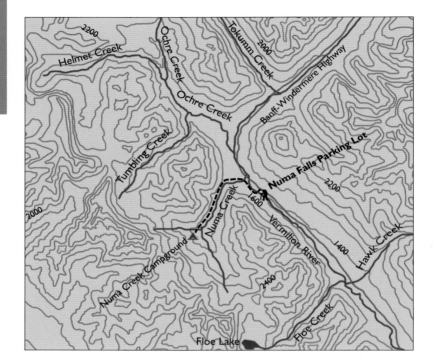

that shortly proceeds back downward. Numa Creek is below on the right side, and the sudden descent quickly brings you to the riverside, and eventually to another metal bridge at the 3-km mark. The flat path continues to stick to the river, crossing many feeder streams, for about 2 km, but will eventually begin a short climb again.

The trail ambles up and down as it parallels the creek and will cross yet another bridge in due course. At the end of this particular crossing, the path levels out and travels through tent pads that lie beside and away from the creek. As much as this may appear to be a campground, do not be fooled; this is not it. Keep on the trail for a bit of an uphill climb and you will run into a sign that sends you straight to the campground with only 400 m remaining.

The campground occupies both banks of a feeder stream that helps fill the waters of Numa Creek. There are bear lockboxes, outhouses, eating areas and campsites on both sites, establishing quite a unique setup. Metal bear boxes replace traditional bear poles due to the increased frequency of *Ursus horribilis* traffic in the area. Numa Creek rushes in from the south and the tributary joins it just south of the campground.

Day trips beyond the campground include Numa Pass, Tumbling Pass and Floe Lake. All of these side trips constitute significant elevation gain, with moderate distances. The Rockwall Trail is just 430 m beyond the campground. Numa Pass is 7.4 km south of the intersection, climbing 833 m from Numa Creek Campground, and Floe Lake is 2.6 km from the pass. The route to Floe Lake drops by 348 m. By contrast, Tumbling Pass, 5.3 km north of the intersection, has an elevation gain of 719 m. Either venture is worthy of the effort but quite exhausting. Or you could just sit in the campground and listen to the streams.

Looking west toward The Rockwall on the trek to the Numa Creek campground.

11. SIMPSON RIVER TRAIL/SURPRISE CREEK CAMPGROUND

This is a lengthy hike with very little elevation change, and compared to other hikes in the area, it has fewer natural landmarks. For the most part, it does as the title suggests: it is a trail that follows the Simpson River. The burnt forest from the Mount Shanks forest fire in 2001 allows scenic viewing not possible through the normally dense forest that would otherwise be here. Although the route begins in Kootenay National Park, the destination at the Surprise Creek shelter and campground lies within the borders of Mount Assiniboine Provincial Park in British Columbia. So make sure you pay your camping fees for the appropriate park.

The shelter is first-come, first-served, and overflow camping is on non-designated pads in the meadow beside the shelter. Because of this system, it is advisable to bring a tent and not depend on the availability of the shelter. The metal bear boxes outside the shelter are to be used by tenters too, not just by shelter occupants. More details are at www.env.gov.bc.ca/bcparks/explore/parkpgs/mt_assiniboine.

DIFFICULTY ▲ ▲ ▲ ▲
DISTANCE: 10.6 KM
ELEVATION GAIN: 175 M

Trailhead:	GPS: N50 58 42.5 W115 56 53.7
	Elevation: 1235 m
Surprise Creek Shelter and Campground:	GPS: N50 58 04.3 W115 49 17.9
	Elevation: 1410 m

Trailhead: The large highway sign marking the Simpson River Trail is 46.8 km down the Banff–Windermere Highway (Hwy. 93) from Castle Junction and 6 km south of Vermilion Crossing. The gravel pullover is on the east (left) side of the parkway, with minimal parking. The pleasant setting of Vermilion Crossing contains the Kootenay Park Lodge, Kootenay Park Visitor Centre and a day-use picnic area.

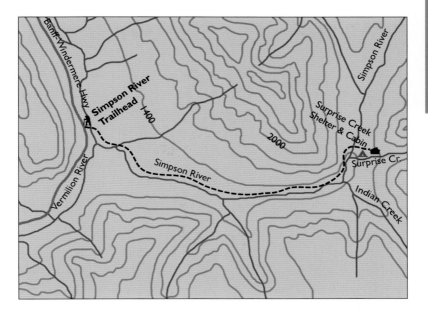

From the trailhead, cross the steel bridge over the Vermilion River to access the backcountry route and the forest of burnt spruce and pine. The long-lasting effects of the fire that ravaged this area are immediately evident and will continue through most of the hike. Once more, due to the minimal blockage by the burnt-out forest, you can see Hawk Ridge directly ahead of you, due east.

You'll see a marker sign, the first of many to come, within the first couple of minutes. The straight line will take you down the Mount Shanks Trail, with a marked distance of 6.9 km. This same sign will direct you to make a 90° right turn to the desired Simpson River Trail. The sign is a tad confusing, as it states that it is 8.6 km to the "SIMPSON RIVER TRAIL," when 8.6 km is actually the distance to the boundary of Kootenay National Park and Mount Assiniboine Provincial Park. The Surprise Creek shelter and campground are in fact 10.6 km away.

During the next 15 to 20 minutes you'll cross numerous minor streams with an easy stride on a path that remains flat and open. For almost 2 km of enjoyable, wide open vistas, the trail and the Simpson River almost touch. The route then rises momentarily above the river, only to succumb to the river's trance once more to parallel it for another ten minutes before climbing above it again.

With the river meandering below for the next half-hour or so, its proximity varies but it is always within earshot. Up here, as you venture farther into the backcountry, the already narrow path becomes even slimmer, though it widens temporarily at a major creek crossing an hour and a half into the journey. The log bridge at this crossing permits views even more spectacular. From the openness of the stream crossing, the hike moves away from the Simpson River and continues to wander up high for another 20 minutes until gently, almost unnoticeably, dropping back down to the river.

Gradually, the trail brings the river closer and parallels it for an additional 20 minutes. As it does this, the route becomes trapped in the incredibly damaged forest, with a high escarpment flanking its left and the Simpson River on its right. This makes for an interesting, narrow, flat flood plain with no escape during flood season, and the terrain through these lowlands can be boggy even in mid-summer. Slowly the trail begins to climb until it eventually settles high above the Simpson River.

Within 10 or 15 minutes, once you're up on the plateau, the river becomes distant and unheard. The scorched forest transitions into a beautiful, lush Rocky Mountain landscape of mature spruce and pine, and you come to the first of many boardwalks. Continue up here through gorgeous forest along many boardwalks over moist ground until you reach the boundary between Mount Assiniboine Provincial Park and Kootenay National Park. The landmark itself presents with minimal fanfare – just a simple mileage post marking the line. However, there is a swath cut straight through the forest as far as you can see. It seems that the boundary required marking by removing a 10-metre-wide strip of forest.

Two easy kilometres remain to be explored before you reach the Surprise Creek shelter and campground. Not much changes, as the river continues to follow the path but remains far below. The main change along the route now is that the forest becomes significantly richer as mosses and ferns dominate the understorey, necessitating the construction of many more boardwalks. Thirty minutes of intermittent boardwalking finally brings the trail back down to the Simpson River. The shelter and campground are reached by crossing a secure, lengthy suspension bridge over the river.

This tranquil setting is unique. On a cloudless evening, the uncluttered, exposed meadow beside the cabin is a far cry finer than spending the night in the cabin's dark, dingy interior.

The closest day hike is a 9-km jaunt to Rock Lake that entails a moderate elevation gain of 608 m. The route is clearly marked at the Surprise Creek area and the path has no obstacles. This is simply a steady uphill climb to the trail and lake.

Simpson River Trail history

James Hector gave the name Simpson to a river, a pass, a ridge and a mountain in honour of the governor of the Hudson's Bay Company, Sir George Simpson. In 1841 Simpson visited the region that later, in 1920, would become Kootenay National Park. He was the first white man on record to visit the area and did so while on a more monumental adventure of attempting to circumnavigate the planet in record time. He followed the Simpson River to its meeting with the Vermilion, travelled down the Kootenay River and crossed through what is now Sinclair Pass, finally ending up at the Columbia River. Needless to say, Simpson did not linger here for long, although he surely loved the scenery.

Hector took time to stop and smell the flowers, though, particularly a wildflower called *Bryanthus empetriformis*. At the summit of Simpson Pass, he discovered this species of pink flowering heath which he compared to "… the very heather of the Highlands of Scotland." Another discovery, maybe not quite so pleasant or beautiful, was his run-in with deerflies as quoted in Brink and Bown's book *Forgotten Highways*:

> We made another discovery, about which there can be no mistake, in a troublesome and venomous species of winged insect, which in size and appearance might have been taken for a cross between the bull-dog and the house fly.

James Hector led an offshoot of the Palliser Expedition into the north end of Kootenay Park in 1858 with the hope of discovering the source of the Bow River and a possible pass as a trading route to the Columbia. It was during this journey that he gave the name Simpson Pass to honour the man who was the first European to visit both this area and present-day Banff. It was on this same trip that Hector was kicked in the chest by an ornery horse and was left for dead. Through an extraordinary recovery, he was able to continue his travels for many more years. A river in the region of the incident was hence named the Kicking Horse River.

George Simpson was born in 1786 or 1787 in Lochbroom, Scotland, and was raised by his father's sister, Mary Simpson. Simpson achieved tremendous business administration experience at a young age when he found employment in London with a company of sugar brokers. With only limited education, and no experience in the fur trade, he achieved overwhelming success. Through perseverance, hard work, an unparalleled hardiness in the wilderness and a few lucky breaks, Simpson eventually became governor of the Hudson's Bay Company, making him one of the most powerful men in British North America at that time.

Mount Assiniboine history

This beautiful peak was named in 1885 by Dr. G.M. Dawson, for the Native people of the area. This was a bit of a faux pas by Dawson, however, since the Assiniboine people were not the region's permanent residents but only hunted in this peaceful part of the Ktunaxa (Kootenay) Indians' territory.

Two years before, Tom Wilson had led Chicago businessman Robert L. Barrett to the base of the mountain by way of Healy Creek, Simpson Pass, Ferro Pass and finally down into the Mitchell River Valley.

George M. Dawson, a geologist, anthropologist, author, teacher, civil servant, geographer and paleontologist was born in Nova Scotia and schooled at McGill (then college) in Montreal, the Royal School of Mines in London and the Geological Survey of Great Britain. While Dawson was teaching chemistry at Morrin College in Quebec City in 1872, a position opened with the Geological Survey of Canada and he obtained it.

He first came to the Rockies in 1884 as leader of a team assembled by the British Association for the Advancement of Science.

In the summer of 1901, James Outram and his climbing companions Christian Bohren and Christian Hasler became the first party to climb to the summit of Mount Assiniboine. The first solo ascent was made by Lawrence Grassie in 1925.

Simpson River. Kootenay National Park

The thinned-out forest from the Mount Shanks fire of 2001.

Surprise Creek shelter. Mount Assiniboine Provincial
Park. Although it is a great refuge during poor weather,
this shelter has a dark and dank interior. I recommend
the campground on a hot summer evening.

Surprise Creek "campground." Mount Assiniboine
Provincial Park.

12. VERDANT CREEK CAMPGROUND

For the initial 5.6 km of this hike, the route progresses through scorched forest as it climbs to its uppermost point at Honeymoon Pass. Beyond the pass, the trail reveals a fascinating, spacious valley, then descends gradually for 2.9 km to Verdant Creek Campground. The creek that shadows the journey is commonly mistaken as Verdant Creek, but it is actually a nameless stream that drains from Verdant Creek near the campground. The adventure through the upper valley is not a simple downhill stroll. There are several stream crossings that are only improvised log bridges, and in some instances there are no bridges at all. Jumping, rockhopping or fording is required.

DIFFICULTY ▲ ▲ ▲ ▲
DISTANCE: 8.5 KM
ELEVATION GAIN: TO HONEYMOON PASS: 699 M
                  TO VERDANT CREEK CAMPGROUND: 503 M

Trailhead: GPS: N51 01 36.9 W115 59 03.7
                               Elevation: 1277 m

Verdant Creek Campground: GPS: N51 04 03.7 W115 56 47.2
                               Elevation: 1780 m

Trailhead: From the intersection of the Trans-Canada Highway and the Banff–Windermere Highway (Hwy. 93) at Castle Junction, travel south into beautiful British Columbia. At the 41.3-km mark, the trailhead for Verdant Creek Campground is on the left (east) side of the highway. It is well marked and is just north of Kootenay Park Lodge. There is a designated parking lot, with a marked trailhead.

The route begins in thin coniferous forest but soon becomes enveloped in the scorched reminder of the 2003 wildfire season. Although substantial forest-floor regrowth has begun, the trees themselves still appear lifeless. As with most trails in this region, this one presents a unique experience of openness within closed forest.

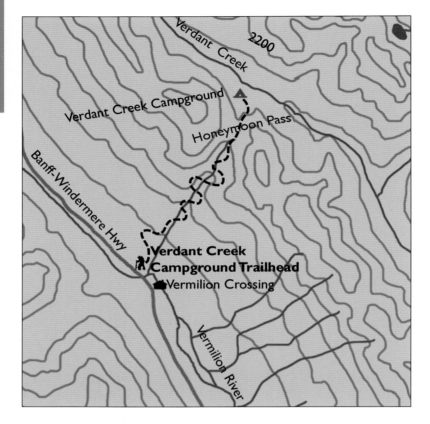

Within five minutes, the trek has transformed from vivid green to shades of charcoal and grey, a stream has been crossed and the hike has begun to climb. The creek travels persistently alongside for the first half of the route as the trail attempts to leave it behind.

Two kilometres into the hike, you'll encounter the first of two series of serious switchbacks, lasting about ten minutes. The second sequence occurs after a five-minute break of level walking. Twenty minutes of relentless climbing brings you to a crossing over the same outlet stream you crossed at the start of this journey. Here, the trail has gained 388 m of the 699 m elevation of Honeymoon Pass. The path becomes increasingly overgrown as it travels farther into the backcountry, with the burnt forest thinning out even more. With less shade, and more sunlight seeping through the forest canopy, the forest floor has become overgrown with wildflowers, small shrubs and grasses. After crossing the creek, the hike climbs at an easy, uphill pace without the monotony of switchbacks.

Ninety minutes and 5.6 km from the trailhead, you reach Honeymoon Pass. The vastness of the upper valley appears stunning, as the route suddenly feels as though it is popping out of the narrow pass. Amazing panoramas of the Ball Range are visible to the northeast.

The trail descends 200 m from the pass to the campground 2.9 km away. The path is easy but fraught with multiple creek crossings over bridges commonly made of narrow logs. The valley floor can be quite mushy, too, as marshes reappear throughout after recent rain. Be careful. The campground is primitive, without an outhouse or a bear pole. Take along some rope to hang your food in a nearby tree.

Kootenay history

Unlike Banff, Lake Louise, Glacier and Revelstoke national parks, Kootenay's beginnings were not influenced by the CPR. This region, with its passes and rivers, was used for trading routes and hunting grounds long before the eventual formation of the park and even longer before the first Europeans arrived.

For centuries the various First Nations had an established economy that integrated trade among them, with some of those relationships spanning great distances. When fur trade by Europeans began to take root in the West, their companies, largely the Hudson's Bay Company and the North West Company, depended almost entirely on Natives to harvest the fur for trade.

The Shuswap and Ktunaxa (Kootenay) Indians were using routes through the Kootenay Park region to trade with the Stoneys across the Rockies as early as the 1700s. And though Europeans later claimed to have discovered these trails, the Natives had already been using them to trade fur with the white man for at least 40 years before white men began using these routes themselves, early in the 19th century.

David Thompson of the North West Company crossed Howse Pass a year after his scouting party, led by Jacques Finlay, bushwhacked the route for him. Thompson had left the relative comfort of Rocky Mountain House on May 10, 1807, and arrived at what they thought was the Blaeberry River on June 30, 1807. As it turned out, they were mistaken and the river was in fact the Columbia, near present-day Invermere. As river travel was quicker and simpler than hiking overland, it was here that Thompson and his party spent a week building boats to continue their exploration. They paused their adventure on July 18, 1807, on the shores of Lake Windermere, where they built log structures they called "Kootenae House" to fend off the upcoming winter and the local Natives.

Although he spent the winter of 1807/08 trading with the Ktunaxa and Shuswap Indians, Thompson did not actually ever venture into the Vermilion or Kootenay watersheds. He came close, and he was in contact with the inhabitants of the territory, but he never set foot into this spectacular eminence of present-day Kootenay National Park.

In 1841 Sir George Simpson became the first non-Native official to set foot in the gorgeous Vermilion drainage system and Kootenay River Valley. Although he was governor of the Hudson's Bay Company at the time, he was not here on official business. Simpson was on a rapid journey around the world that took him to this region as a through-hiker only; he barely had time to stop and smell the flowers. The river he discovered while on his record-breaking attempt around the globe was named after him in 1858 by Palliser Expedition leader James Hector. Simpson is also the first recorded person to soak in Radium Hot Springs. Apparently, he bathed in a pool that was just large enough to hold one man. Radium Hot Springs would become a major influence in convincing governments to build the Banff–Windermere Highway and to constitute Kootenay National Park.

Later in the same year as Simpson passed through, James Sinclair visited the area as a guide, bringing 23 Red River Métis families to the Columbia River from Winnipeg (then called Fort Garry). They then followed the Columbia to Walla Walla, Washington. Sinclair contracted this favour for the Hudson's Bay Company even though he was not directly employed by them at the time. Sinclair travelled the same passage as

Simpson, entering the Vermilion district to the Kootenay River, coming over White Man Pass and eventually through another pass that would ultimately bear his name. The Hudson's Bay Company was attempting to gain a presence in the Washington and Oregon territories, and Sinclair's emigration was a part of this plan. He was put in charge of trade and restoration of Fort Walla Walla in 1853. During an Indian uprising in 1855, Walla Walla was sacked and looted. Fortunately, Sinclair and his party had been ordered to depart just prior to the attack. Nonetheless, he met his demise on March 26, 1856, during an Indian attack on the Cascade Locks settlement, in Oregon.

Four years later a Belgian-born missionary began an arduous adventure that would carry him from Lake Pend Oreille, Idaho, to the Bow River Valley near Canmore, Alberta. The purpose of Father Pierre-Jean de Smet's trek was to meet and convert the Natives along his route, which he did when he finally assembled with the Chippewa, Cree and Blackfoot in the Canmore region. The direction de Smet took on this endeavour was more or less the reverse of the path taken by James Sinclair in 1841. There is some speculation as to his exact route, however. According to Dr. George M. Dawson, a member of the Geological Survey of Canada, de Smet ventured up the Columbia River to the Kootenay by way of Sinclair Pass, then down the Kootenay to the Cross River. He completed his voyage by following the Cross upstream, finally going over White Man Pass into present-day Canmore. Apparently, the Cross River derives its name from a cross that de Smet erected at some point along the river.

All was quiet through here for another 13 years until the accidental arrival of James Hector of the Palliser Expedition in 1858. Dr. Hector had been sent from Old Bow Fort, near present-day Morley, Alberta, to explore the Bow Valley and search for the source of the Bow River. He was guided by a Stoney Indian, Nimrod, who drew a map of the route that Hector should take to find his objective. The map, incidentally, put Hector and his crew on an indirect course, finally coming out of Vermilion Pass, which is today's Banff–Windermere Highway (Hwy. 93).

The Palliser Expedition leader named many of the features in the Vermilion and Kootenay basins, including Mount Ball, the Blaeberry

River, Castle Mountain, Goodsir Towers, the Purcell Range and Simpson Pass. During his time through here, Hector also found the source of the Vermilion River and the point of its entry into the Kootenay, and followed the Beaverfoot River from the Kootenay to discover the Kicking Horse River (see "Simpson River Trail" for the origin of the name of the Kicking Horse River).

The renowned British mountaineer Edward Whymper arrived in Canada in 1901 at the request of the CPR, which wanted him to help promote the Rocky Mountain adventures and luxuries the CPR was marketing in Britain and Europe. Whymper and his entourage of guides Joseph Pollinger, Christian Klucker, Christian Kaufmann (Kaufmann Lake) and Joseph Bossonney explored the Rockies, Selkirks and Vermilion areas and ascended several of their peaks, including Mount Whymper and Stanley Peak. Soon after this well-publicized exploration, outfitters like Walter Nixon began guiding tourists through these valleys on horseback, blazing many of the trails that are still used today.

In the early 1880s, a settler named John McKay homesteaded in the present-day Radium Hot Springs, staking a claim along the Columbia River, which included the springs. He did nothing to develop the springs, however, and by 1890 a British entrepreneur named Roland Stuart paid $1 per acre for a Crown grant of the 160 acres containing the pool. Stuart's original plan was to sell bottled water, as it was believed to have medicinal minerals, but when analysis of the water in 1913 revealed the presence of radium, he changed course and began developing a spa that would rival the famous one at Bath, England.

After the initial construction of the bathhouse and pools, Stuart departed for England to join up for the First World War. Before he could return, the federal and British Columbia governments expropriated the land in 1920 for $40,000 as part of the negotiations for the Banff–Windermere Highway. The value of the springs was judged by some to be more in the neighbourhood of $500,000.

Construction of the highway from the Columbia Valley had begun in 1911, but the war put construction on hold. The war left the British Columbia government penniless and unable to complete the highway, so the federal government decided to finish it, with the stipulation that the provincial government turn over a five-mile corridor of land on either side of the highway for a national park.

The forest into the Verdant Creek campground shows advanced signs of recovery from the 2003 forest fire season. Extensive meadows of beautiful wildflowers now populate what was once a forest of spruce and pine.

The overwhelming view of The Rockwall from Honeymoon Pass.

13. KINNEY LAKE CAMPGROUND

The walk to Kinney Lake explores a rare Rocky Mountain environment, as this area is one of only a few interior rain forests in the province. This phenomenon is due mainly to the sheer size of Mount Robson. Passing clouds from Pacific disturbances are held here, intensifying precipitation. Huge red cedars are abundant among Douglas fir, hemlock and spruce. Club moss, spike moss, ferns, lady's slipper and wild lily of the valley carpet the forest floor. The Robson River offers a bounty of views throughout this hike, as the route seldom strays from it. This campground is the first one on the 22-km Berg Lake Trail. The Berg Lake is one of the most spectacular treks in the entire Rocky Mountain park system and is by far my favourite. Because of the low elevation, the Berg Lake Trail is usually the first route in the Rockies to become snow free in spring. It is busy, so make reservations.

DIFFICULTY ▲ ▲
DISTANCE: 6.7 KM
ELEVATION GAIN: 132 M

Trailhead: GPS: N53 03 01.7 W119 12 52.6
                                    Elevation: 839 m

Kinney Lake Campground: GPS: N53 05 13.3 W119 11 43.0
                                    Elevation: 971 m

Trailhead: From Jasper, Alberta, the Mount Robson Visitor Centre is a straightforward, picturesque 85-km drive west on Hwy. 16. From the west, the trailhead is 35 km from Valemount, BC, though when leaving Valemount you must first head north on Hwy. 5 for 20 km and then turn right (east) onto Hwy. 16. Drive the remaining 15 km on Hwy. 16 to the visitor centre. From the visitor centre, turn right, onto Kinney Lake Road, heading north. Travel along the paved frontage road for 2 km to the Berg Lake trailhead parking lot. Park, strap on your backpack and cross the bridge over the Robson River to reach the trailhead.

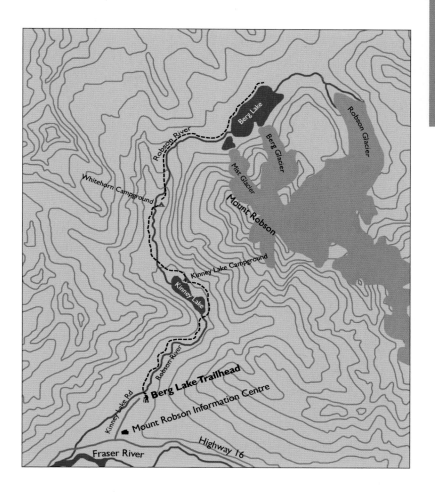

The spacious path provides a gentle, unobstructed hike along the busiest trail system in the Rocky Mountain park system. An avalanche slope is exposed at km 1, a reminder of how dynamic these otherwise stable giants can be. This expanse of openness is the first of two rises before arriving at Kinney Lake Campground, but with only 70 m of elevation gain over 500 m it is quite effortless. Before the track fades back into the forest at the top of this knoll, there is a dazzling view of Mt. Robson, straight up the way.

The wide trail, wide enough to walk side by side, meanders through a magnificent old-growth forest of Douglas fir, cedar, hemlock and spruce. The sight of these huge trees is breathtaking. They are truly glorious. This is unlike any forest in the Rocky Mountain park system. Even the damp odours from the ferns, mosses, lichens and fungi are exceptional. These natural surroundings remain unchanged until you reach the bridge over the Kinney Lake outlet at the 4.5-km mark. This tranquil setting is a popular spot to stop and rest, as the serene, fast, yet smoothly flowing stream quickly becomes intoxicating. Or maybe it is just popular because there's an outhouse in the forest on the other side of the bridge.

Back into the lush forest, the path narrows as it sidesteps the lake. Another kilometre along, the second rise on this route begins to climb through a series of switchbacks. The trail to the Kinney Lake viewpoint intersects to the left partway through this modest elevation gain. It is worth the momentary detour along a well-constructed boardwalk to observe the lake from this precipice. The hike continues to ascend briefly, levels out, then descends to the lakeside once again.

The approach to the campground spans an outwash pan of sand and gravel. This entanglement of streams can present a minor inconvenience during high glacial runoff and you should utilize the wooden platforms provided for this crossing. Tent pads are available along the shoreline entering the campground that can be used to offset the effects of a hot summer day. More-protected tent pads are at hand in the forest surrounding the main campground. The common campsite area opens up with an impressive shelter at its heart that functions as a cooking area and meeting place. Splendid lakeside viewing is offered here along this treeless shoreline.

Kinney Lake is an archetypal glacier-fed lake, owing its aquamarine hue to its purity, enabling short-wavelength light to be reflected off tiny mineral particles ground by glaciers. The valley that this dazzling lake resides in was gouged out by retreating ice during the late Pleistocene period of glaciation, 30,000 to 21,000 years ago. As the ice melted, the resulting water filled gouged-out low spots to form the lake. Today, the lake's source resides in the Robson glacial system: the combined Berg,

Mist and Robson glaciers on the north rampart of Mount Robson. This system also nourishes Berg Lake and the Robson River. Directly across Kinney Lake, Cinnamon Peak and Whitehorn Mountain to the north (right) rise to confine the southwest shore of the lake. Drainage from snowpack in these mountains produces waterfalls that cascade hundreds of metres down the rock walls and into the lake.

Day trips from the campground depend on your stamina. The only direction is to go farther up the trail. This and much more about Berg Lake are discussed in the Whitehorn Campground chapter, next.

Kinney Lake, looking southeast on the way to Whitehorn Campground. Glacial and snowpack runoff from Berg Lake and from Berg, Mist and Robson glaciers crash through the Valley of a Thousand Falls to gently settle into Kinney Lake.

Toboggan Falls. Located above the Berg Lake campground, Toboggan provides a full day of exploration.

14. WHITEHORN CAMPGROUND

The mapping points for the Whitehorn Campground adventure comprise the entire distance of the route, while the description starts as you leave Kinney Lake Campground (page 94). The hike to Kinney Lake is a superb 6.7-km trek through a wonderful old-growth forest. From Kinney Lake, the route to Whitehorn Campground becomes rather laborious, as there are two miserable sections with significant elevation gain. But the astonishing scenery soon relieves the misery of zigzagging higher and higher. I really hope you love this trek as much as I do.

DIFFICULTY ▲ ▲ ▲
DISTANCE: 10.9 KM
ELEVATION GAIN: 286 M

FROM KINNEY LAKE CAMPGROUND:
DISTANCE: 4.2 KM
ELEVATION GAIN: 154 M

Trailhead:	GPS: N53 03 01.7 W119 12 52.6
	Elevation: 839 m
Kinney Lake Campground:	GPS: N53 05 13.3 W119 11 43.0
	Elevation: 971 m
Whitehorn Campground:	GPS: N53 06 33.4 W119 12 42.5
	Elevation: 1125 m

Trailhead: The Mount Robson Visitor Centre is 35 km east of Valemount, BC, and 85 km west of Jasper, Alberta, on Hwy. 16. The village of Valemount is situated along Hwy. 5, 20 km south of the Hwy. 16/Hwy. 5 junction. Turn right and head west at the crossroad to complete the remaining 15 km. The trailhead is 2 km north from the visitor centre, at the end of Kinney Lake Road.

Start out from the north end of Kinney Lake Campground and head into the woods. The route is pleasantly flat for 300 m, and you come to a bicycle drop-off area at a fork in the trail. Riding bicycles is permitted only up to this point, where a metal rack provides secure lockup. A bypass route leaves to the right into the forest here as well. Early in the season, on the delta plain flats below, the feeder streams supplying Kinney Lake run high and forceful, but the path running to the right bypasses the flats and all of the excessive runoff. Do not take the left trail leading to the flats unless you have checked with the Mount Robson Information Centre about the condition of the flats. Even if you're travelling late in the season and water levels are low, remnants of the destructive force of high flows may linger in the form of washed-out bridges.

The trail to the right travels through undulating forest with such high, steep banks that you should be extra cautious. Falling from these heights could be fatal. The route rolls through the forest of hemlock and spruce for 1.5 km and then suddenly drops to join once more with the wide, flat delta at 8.2 km. You'll cross some interesting channels down here over sturdy, permanent aluminum bridges. Some 10 to 15 minutes of wandering the flats takes you to the 9-km mark, at the base of a series of switchbacks. The alluvial plain is unique enough to deserve some extra time. The scenery is enormous, as there is nothing to block your view of peaks, waterfalls, limestone walls and green forest.

You gain 154 m over the next magnificent kilometre. The beauty of Kinney Lake with the backdrop of Campion Mountain makes the climb barely noticeable. The mountainside ascent reaches its zenith after this gain, then re-enters the trees and begins to ramble up and down. At 10.9 km, a wooden suspension bridge crosses the Robson River to Whitehorn Campground.

This spot is a common base for progressing up the endless switchbacks to Berg Lake. Many day trippers camp at Whitehorn and continue upward for a full day the following day. Reaching the next campground, at Emperor Falls 5 km away, will take 531 m of gruelling elevation gain. Then the trail levels off almost completely for another 5 km to attain Berg Lake Campground. However, the prizes – Berg Lake, Mount Robson, the moraines and glaciers – can be seen clearly from Marmot Campground, 8 km from Whitehorn.

This is indeed a full day, but the beauty is incomparable. The valley beyond Whitehorn is called the Valley of a Thousand Falls. Although a thousand may be a stretch, there is nothing else like this in the Rocky Mountain parks, and possibly on earth. I have taken this trip well over 20 times simply because of the unique diversity and immeasurable magnificence. I have sat in Berg Lake Campground on a clear day, my back against a tree, just gazing at Berg Lake and Mount Robson for hours.

Lurking around Whitehorn Campground is certainly a fascinating day, with trips down to the far north end along the flat, wide banks of the Robson River. Venturing back to the suspension bridge and over to the rocky banks in front of the warden cabin reveals cold pools alive with surging springs, most likely caused by the pressure of the raging river.

Robson history

Arthur Coleman named the exquisitely beautiful Kinney Lake in 1907. As he put it in his book *The Canadian Rockies*:

> Through the bush along the river our loads were an immense nuisance, but presently we reached the forks, and then had good going on the shore of a beautiful lake, which had been visited by Mr. Kinney the day before, and has been named Lake Kinney in honour of our indefatigable comrade.

The stunning beauty of Kinney Lake and the entire Mount Robson area were a secondary discovery to the original pursuit of summiting Mount Robson. Still, Kinney Lake, Whitehorn, Valley of a Thousand Falls, Toboggan Falls, Snowbird Pass and Berg and Hargreaves lakes were all magnificent finds by themselves.

Arthur Philemon Coleman, a professor of geology from the University of Toronto, his brother, L. Quincy Coleman, a rancher from Morley, Alberta, and L.B. Stewart, also a professor from the University of Toronto, all set out in the summer of 1893 to find and climb the tallest mountains in North America. For 66 years there had been a legend floating around that mounts Hooker and Brown, in the Athabasca Pass region, reached heights of between 15,000 and 17,000 feet above sea level. After discovering that those peaks were not even close to such a height (Mount Brown is a mere 9,184 feet, while Mount Hooker is slightly taller at 10,781 feet), the Coleman brothers headed for what is now known as Mount Robson in an attempt to hunt down a first ascent of history-making height. In 1907, they departed Lake Louise in search of this legendary peak, and this time, unlike with mounts Brown and Hooker, they would not be disappointed. The reports of a mountain of over 10,000 feet high proved to be underestimated, as Mount Robson rises to 12,973 feet.

A.O. Wheeler had prompted the Colemans to make the journey and arranged to have Reverend George Kinney, a clergyman and mountaineering guide, enlist with the group. The trek from Lake Louise took 39 days, leaving them with supplies for only one attempt, which ultimately failed. It was during this attempt that they came upon Kinney Lake, camping by its shore and using it as a base for this first attempt on Robson. Returning the following year, the same party left from Edmonton, this time with the addition of guide John Yates. During the journey, A.P. Coleman sprained his knee, temporarily suspending his climbing skills.

The following June, Kinney set off alone, once again from Edmonton, "… hoping to pick up someone on the trail to share fortune with me." While in Jasper waiting for the Athabasca River's swollen waters to subside, he met Donald "Curly" Phillips, a member of the Guide Association of Ontario. Phillips had come to Jasper to start an outfitting business, but was now on his way to ascending the most elusive summit in the Canadian Rockies. On Friday, August 13, 1909, after enduring hard travel, bad weather and dwindling supplies, they finally summited Mount Robson.

The accomplishment, however, was tarnished with controversy and doubt, and without witnesses or convincing, definitive evidence, their claim of first ascent was disputed and finally disallowed. The summit was officially bagged on July 31, 1913, by an ACC-sanctioned climb. The victorious members of that party were Albert McCarthy, Billy Foster and Conrad Kain. A.P. Coleman was a support member of the ACC base camp alongside A.O. Wheeler, Charles Fay and A.L. Mumm.

White Falls is one of many spectacular cascades
that plummet through the Valley of a Thousand Falls
between Kinney Lake and Whitehorn campgrounds.

15. LAUGHING FALLS CAMPGROUND

Backpacking to Laughing Falls is undoubtedly one of the easiest hikes in this guide and should be considered as a warm-up trip or a quest to work the bugs out of newly purchased gear. Having said that, the short trip to Laughing Falls is an extraordinary trek with a couple of notable sights.

DIFFICULTY ▲
DISTANCE: 4.2 KM
ELEVATION GAIN: 96 M

Trailhead:	GPS: N51 30 11.0 W116 29 16.3
	Elevation: 1509 m
Laughing Falls Campground:	GPS: N51 31 50.9 W116 30 25.2
	Elevation: 1605 m

Trailhead: After you obtain a wilderness pass from the Yoho Information Centre in Field, BC, drive 3.7 km east on the Trans-Canada Highway and turn left onto Yoho Valley Road. Follow this road for 13 km to the Takakkaw Falls parking area. The Yoho Valley Trail starts at the far end of the parking lot. Almost immediately after the hike begins, you will reach Takakkaw Falls Campground, barely 400 m from the parking lot. Through the campground, at its far end, is the Yoho Valley trailhead.

Laughing Falls is an easy hike along a relatively flat path that climbs a few gentle slopes. The hike meanders through a forest of pine and spruce, arriving at clearings near the beginning and at the campground. At 2.3 km into the journey is the signed junction for side trails leading to the viewpoints of the lovely Angels Staircase Falls and Point Lace Falls. This stop is well worth the small detour for a spectacular view of both of these captivating falls. When the Yoho Valley Trail continues beyond this point, it climbs 76 m over 1.4 km. This is the only challenging section.

As the path levels off, the short, 400-m side trail leading to Lake Duchesnay is marked, but the trip in actually seems much shorter than

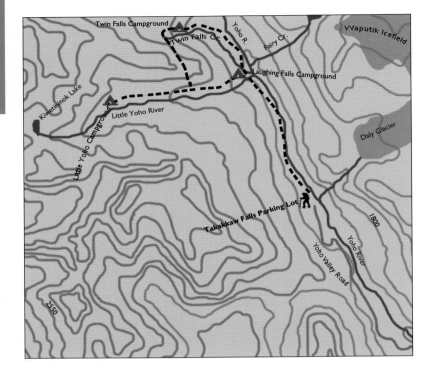

the 400 m indicated by the Parks Canada sign. The lake starts to dry up by late June and is often completely dry by late August. Don't let your sense of adventure get carried away here, as the mud can often be knee-deep. From this intersection, the level path crosses the Little Yoho River and enters Laughing Falls Campground just a few short minutes later.

Laughing Falls Campground is located on an alluvial fan. Campers in this forest clearing enjoy a spectacular view of Yoho Glacier to the north and the Waputik Range to the east. Three streams intersect at the campground: the Yoho and Little Yoho rivers and Twin Falls Creek. The source of the Yoho River and Twin Falls Creek is the massive Wapta Icefield, while the Little Yoho derives its energy from Kiwetinok Lake. There are tent pads along the banks of these streams for those campers who like to drift off to sleep to the sound of rushing water. To reach the captivating and accessible Laughing Falls, cross the bridge that leads to the campground, stay left and follow the well-beaten path to the viewpoint.

The best day excursion from Laughing Falls Campground is the rustic Twin Falls Teahouse, 4.3 km farther up the trail. The first phase of the teahouse was constructed by the Canadian Pacific Railway in 1908 as a single-storey cabin for overnight backcountry touring. An additional storey was finished in 1924, adding room for more guests. Simple meals and beverages are offered throughout the summer. The teahouse derives its name from the extraordinary Twin Falls situated at this remarkable landscape. The top of the waterfall is split in two by a large limestone block, after which the two cascades merge into one as the water plummets 180 m into a narrow gorge.

Yoho history

James Hector was the first non-Native explorer to reach these lands, in 1858. He departed Old Bow Fort on August 11 of that year to explore the Bow Valley and search for the source of the Bow River. After initially coming to this region of beauty as a member of the Palliser Expedition, Hector had expanded his exploration and would end up seeking a trading route to the Columbia River. He was guided by a Stoney Indian, Nimrod, who had a rough map of the route he had decided Hector should take as he left Old Bow Fort. The map, incidentally, put Hector and his crew on an indirect course that had them finally coming out of Vermilion Pass. During the exploration into the Kootenai area, Hector discovered the Kicking Horse River.

It would be some years before the Kicking Horse/Yoho area began to see more visitors. The town of Field was established in 1880, resulting from an influx of CPR construction workers. The townsite of tents and shacks became a hub of activity and soon small outbuildings began to crop up, including hotels, guide houses and chalets. Hiking trails were also constructed, to entice tourists as well as investors and help ensure economic success for the new enterprise. Many of the routes still used today were constructed during this time. The railway was completed in 1885, and to further stimulate tourism to this gorgeous place the CPR introduced Swiss guides to escort amateur mountaineers to the surrounding summits.

The CPR's marketing efforts were successful, and to accommodate the resulting influx of tourists the company progressively constructed an ensemble of lodges in the present-day Yoho area. Facilities were completed at Emerald Lake, Lake O'Hara, Wapta Lake and in the Yoho Valley. The pride of these lodges was Mount Stephen House, completed in 1886. It was initially built as a dining hall so that trains did not have to haul heavy diner-cars up the steep grade to Field. Converted to a YMCA hostel during the First World War, Mount Stephen House never regained its former glory, and by 1963 it had been dismantled.

The Yoho Valley was finally explored in 1896/97 by a mathematics professor from Berlin, Jean Habel, who had climbed extensively in the Andes and the Alps. Habel was the first to discover the headwaters of the Athabasca River. Habel Creek in Jasper National Park is named after him. He also claimed to have discovered Takakkaw Falls, Yoho Pass, Emerald Lake and the Yoho Glacier, though the noted guide, outfitter and prospector Tom Wilson later attempted to discredit those claims at least in part, asserting that it was he and not Habel who had discovered Emerald Lake and Yoho Pass.

Angels Staircase Falls. Yoho National Park.

16. TWIN FALLS CAMPGROUND

This is a wonderful enhancement to the Laughing Falls Campground stroll (page 103). Considering that the trek into Laughing Falls is quite short and has very little change in elevation, extending the trip another 2.5 km without a gain in altitude may seem reasonable. Factors such as weather, darkness and attitude all come in to play. The trail is level, smooth and dry, with only a couple of stretches that may require some work.

DIFFICULTY ▲ ▲
DISTANCE: 6.7 KM
ELEVATION GAIN: 99 M

Trailhead:	GPS: N51 30 11.0 W116 29 16.3
	Elevation: 1509 m
Laughing Falls Campground	GPS: N51 31 50.9 W116 30 25.2
	Elevation: 1605 m
Twin Falls Campground:	GPS: N51 32 43.5 W116 31 24.2
	Elevation: 1608 m

Trailhead: Drive 3.7 km east on the Trans-Canada Highway from the Yoho National Park Information Centre and turn left onto Yoho Valley Road. Follow this road for 13 km to the Takakkaw Falls parking area. The Yoho Valley Trail starts at the far end of the parking lot. The hike begins by taking you to Takakkaw Falls Campground, situated 400 m from the parking lot. Just beyond is the Yoho Valley trailhead.

The majority of the hike consists of the same trail as to Laughing Falls Campground, so the first 4.2 km is relatively flat and easy. Sideshows along the way include viewing both Angels Staircase Falls and Point Lace Falls 2.3 km into the journey. There is a mild elevation gain of 76 m from here before a fork in the road directs you left to visit Lake Duchesnay. The lake is only a few hundred metres away at best, even though the Parks sign insists it is 400 m. Regardless, the route continues straight past this juncture to Laughing Falls Campground only a few minutes ahead, on the other side of a sturdy steel bridge that crosses the Little Yoho River.

The falls are on the left (west) side of a smooth trail that cuts through the campground. At the far end, you reach another signed intersection guiding you to take the right fork to continue to Twin Falls Campground 2.5 km farther on. The remainder of the route is an enjoyable walk beside Twin Falls Creek with negligible change in altitude.

Shortly after departing Laughing Falls Campground, the path crosses Twin Falls Creek, landing on the eastern bank. The spruce and pine forest is thick, but it occasionally permits partial glimpses of the dual falls. Infrequently, gorgeous hemlocks also populate the Twin Creek Valley. Continue uninterrupted through forest paralleling the creek until you reach the Yoho Glacier junction at the 6.4-km mark. The way is obvious, as the glacier trail branches to the right and the campground sits a short descent down the left fork.

The campground has eight sites, a bear pole and a couple of outhouses. A central cooking area is difficult to locate, but it is there. However, if you are not in the mood for cooking, get back on the trail and climb about 200 m within 1.5 km. If you were not hungry before setting out, you certainly will be when you reach the chalet.

The falls drop 180 m after being split into two cascades by a limestone block. The two falling-water chutes merge just before they land in a narrow chasm. This is an utterly glorious waterfall. The sound, sight and feel of this natural wonder will fill your body with joy. Occasionally, during low glacial runoff seasons, the left passage would become blocked. The recourse was to blast the waterway with dynamite. This was not a permanent solution, however, as I witnessed the single-drop spectacle first-hand in 2003. At first we felt cheated, but soon realized we were being treated to a rare event.

Twin Falls history

A Canadian Pacific Railway crew cut the trail to these falls in 1901 as part of an ongoing drive to develop the Rocky Mountains for tourism. As the popularity of the falls grew, the CPR built the tea house to feed and house guests who had ventured in to see this spectacular site.

The first phase of the teahouse was constructed in 1908 as a single-storey cabin for overnight backcountry touring. In 1915, more effort was directed toward trail construction and the path was greatly augmented. It is this same route that we hike today. The upgrade inspired more visitors and the CPR found itself turning overnight guests away. So eventually, in 1923, the railway leased this idyllic half-acre setting from the National Parks Branch, instituting "Twin Falls Rest," named, of course, for the extraordinary Twin Falls cascade. Construction of an additional storey to the teahouse began in 1922 and was finished in 1924. From 1925 to 1928, the first and second phases were joined together by a simple, single-storey connection.

The teahouse still offers simple meals and beverages throughout the summer.

A very rare sight. Only during extremely dry summers do the dual chutes of Twin Falls consist of only a single cascade.

17. LITTLE YOHO CAMPGROUND

This is a lengthy trip with considerable elevation gain, making the trek into Little Yoho Valley one of the toughest backpacking trips in this guide. The first 4.2 km of this hike takes the same trail as the trip to Laughing Falls Campground (page 103). The beauty of the lower valley of the Laughing Falls route is augmented by the wilderness of the upper regions. As you pop out from a gruelling stretch of switchbacks to be treated to the incredible wonder up there, you will soon realize why you put yourself through so much suffering. The stretch of terrain approaching Little Yoho Valley teases you by providing glimpses of what the valley delivers.

DIFFICULTY ▲ ▲ ▲ ▲
DISTANCE: 9.3 KM
ELEVATION GAIN: 551 M

Trailhead:	GPS: N51 30 11.0 W116 29 16.3
	Elevation: 1509 m
Little Yoho Campground:	GPS: N51 31 36.0 W116 33 48.0
	Elevation: 2060 m

Trailhead: From the Yoho Information Centre in Field, BC, drive 3.7 km east on the Trans-Canada Highway and turn left onto Yoho Valley Road. The parking area for the trailhead is 13 km in, at the Takakkaw Falls parking lot, with the Yoho Valley Trail beginning its journey at the far end of the parking lot. Only five minutes into the hike, just 400 m from the parking lot, you'll come to Takakkaw Falls Campground. The Yoho Valley trailhead is situated at the far end of the campground.

The first section of the hike is to Laughing Falls and is an easy walk along a relatively flat path that climbs a few gentle slopes. The route meanders through a forest of pine and spruce, with clearings near the beginning of the hike and at the campground. At 2.3 km into the journey is the signed junction for side trails leading to the lovely Angels Staircase Falls and Point Lace Falls. This stop is well worth the small detour for a spectacular view of both waterfalls.

Approximately 1.4 km farther along, the short, 400-m side trail leading to Lake Duchesnay is another easy detour. From this intersection, the level path crosses over the Little Yoho River into Laughing Falls Campground just a few short minutes later.

Carry on through the campground to a signed intersection at the far north end. Take the left turn upward to Little Yoho Campground and the Alpine Club of Canada's Stanley Mitchell Hut. Settle in, physically and mentally, for a long haul of constant switchbacks lasting for about a half-hour. Not much else to mention here other than switchbacks: no views, no waterfalls, no glaciers, no tarns, not even a bear. Just switchbacks. You will know when you are close to the end of the agony when you approach a broken-down boardwalk. Be careful, as there are exposed spike heads, and the aged boards are quite slippery.

Just up the way there is a junction and the summit of the switchbacks. Good going. Turn left toward Little Yoho Campground and to another sign saying it's 3.5 km to the campground. The redundancy of signs continues 100 m later directing you to the right with 3.4 km remaining. Although the switchbacks are behind you, the hike continues to climb at a steady, moderate rate. Another kilometre gained and the trees open up in a short clearing exposing towering mountain peaks. But this is just the beginning of the remarkably diverse beauty of the Little Yoho Valley. You are near the end of the trail. As the route levels off, the Little Yoho River runs beside it and the way becomes increasingly open, revealing more spectacular views, including the Iceline to your left (west).

A streamside walk over tributaries and clearings suddenly erupts into the massive meadow and the "community" of Little Yoho. The surroundings will astound you. The Stanley Mitchell Hut is on your immediate right, the warden cabin is to the far left and the campground is directly ahead. This is one of the busiest remote regions in the Canadian Rocky Mountain national park system. The ACC hut can accommodate 26 trekkers, and the campground has ten campsites.

Day hikes include scrambling mounts Kerr and Pollinger; reaching the highest named lake in Canada, Kiwetinok; exploring the Iceline Trail; and backtracking to Twin Falls. It is no wonder that the translation of the Cree word Yoho is "place of wonder." Other renditions might include amazing, awesome and beautiful. This piece of Earth is all of these and more.

The Alpine Club of Canada's Stanley Mitchell Hut is the focal point for explorers of the Little Yoho Valley.

One of many wonders of The Little Yoho Valley is the vast open expanse that provides so many magnificent panoramas.

Looking west, the beauty of Kiwetinok Lake and
Kiwetinok Pass lay nestled ahead in the middle notch,
high above the floor of The Little Yoho Valley.

The Little Yoho Valley is surrounded by some of the
best prizes in the Canadian Rocky Mountains. You
could spend weeks exploring up here.

113

18. YOHO LAKE CAMPGROUND

Of the many approaches to Yoho Lake, the way in from Emerald Lake is the least formidable, as the assault is lengthy yet gradual. Accessing the lake from the Takakkaw Falls parking area consists of a straight, deliberate series of gruelling switchbacks upward. Not a lot of fun. The route from Emerald Lake entails greater overall elevation gain, but it is spread over several more kilometres.

DIFFICULTY ▲ ▲ ▲
DISTANCE: 8 KM
ELEVATION GAIN: 510 M

Trailhead:	GPS: N51 28 29.0 W116 29 06.3
	Elevation: 1306 m
Yoho Pass Summit:	GPS: N51 26 20.0 W116 32 29.2
	Elevation: 1816 m
Yoho Lake Campground:	GPS: N51 28 29.0 W116 29 06.3
	Elevation: 1748 m

Trailhead: Emerald Lake Road is 1.6 km west of the Yoho Information Centre in Field. Turn right onto the road and follow it for 9 km until you reach the Emerald Lake Lodge parking lot.

As you leave the Emerald Lake public parking lot, take the immediate left instead of the bridge over to the lodge. The sign reads Yoho Lake 8.0 km and Yoho Pass 7.3 km. It takes about two to three minutes to depart the paved trail and another 15 to reach the far end of Emerald Lake. A sign directs traffic left to the Emerald Basin; make sure you avoid this fork and stay straight.

Just beyond this junction is a distinct marker sending you to Yoho Lake and Takkakaw Falls. The falls are 10.5 km away, the lake 6.4 km. This is a rather unusual path for the Canadian Rockies, as it is flat and straight for a little over a kilometre, seeming more like a seismic line than a trail.

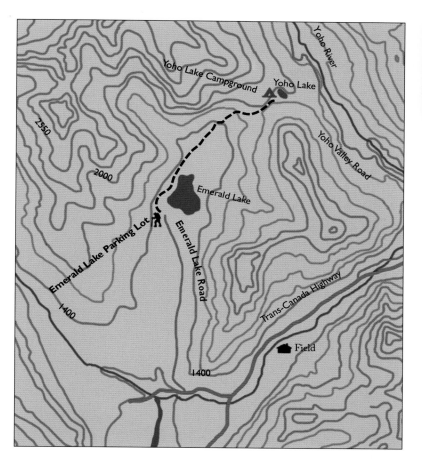

The route travels across an alluvial fan formed by braided streams that have deposited rocks, trees and silt. An alluvial fan typically forms where water from a canyon or gorge enters a flat plain. As the pressure of the flow diminishes, the water slows and spreads across the plain, depositing the silt, trees and rocks it was carrying through the canyon. The gorge in question is evident as you look to the left and follow the source of the alluvial fan. An extensive array of boardwalks traverses the many streams of the fan. Even so, there are some minor rockhops and stream jumping, depending on the extent of runoff during the season.

At the end of the flats, the hike begins its climb toward Yoho Pass. As you approach the switchbacks in the openness of the fan, you get a better perspective of the journey ahead. The degree of the incline becomes evident, as you are faced with nowhere to go but up and over the pass. The switchbacks, as usual, are steep and steady with only a few breaks of level terrain. Look back behind you to see an amazing scene consisting of the alluvial fan, Emerald Lake, mountains of the Van Horne Range and the trail on the flats.

Twenty minutes of climbing brings the route alongside a short, wide waterfall that is close enough to the path that you can feel its spray. On a hot summer day the spray and nearby shade provide a cool, refreshing reprieve. Just a few metres uphill from the falls, the path flattens as it approaches a slope of rubble about a kilometre long. The hike re-enters the forest at the far end of the slope and will ascend another 201 m to the crest of Yoho Pass. From the pass it's only a minor descent of 750 m to the lake.

The setting of Yoho Lake is one of profound tranquility. Day trips from here include the Iceline Trail to Little Yoho Valley and Celeste Lake.

During spring runoff, an elevated trail makes navigating an alluvial fan much more pleasant. This particular boardwalk is along the lower level of the Yoho Lake trail.

The most notable beauty of the Yoho Lake trail is the
abundance of water as it finds its way to Emerald Lake.

Mount Burgess looms high over the silent waters of
Emerald Lake.

117

A spectacular day with matching scenery along the Mount Niles trek. The base of Mount Niles is on the far right.

Chapter 6
Scrambling Trips

1. ABBOTT RIDGE

The Abbott Ridge scramble is an amazing uphill stroll through thick forest that offers very few sights until the path exits the treeline. The forest trail itself, however, even without views, presents wondrous sensations for your senses, as the smell and feel of the forest become increasingly heavy the higher you go. Just before leaving the forest, you pass Marion Lake, offering a respite from steady climbing. Leaving the forest, though, delivers a bounty of viewing pleasures.

DIFFICULTY ▲ ▲ ▲
ELEVATION GAIN: 1106 M

Trailhead:	GPS: N51 15 58.9 W117 29 48.3
	Elevation: 1226 m
Marion Lake:	Elevation: 1707 m
Abbott Ridge Summit:	GPS: N51 14 44.6 W117 30 48.7
	Elevation: 2332 m

Trailhead: The trailhead is located in Illecillewaet Campground's recreation area, 3 km west of the crest of Rogers Pass. This minor exit off the highway is a busy little mecca for campers, hikers, scramblers, climbers, cross-country skiers and picnickers. Enter the campground off the east side of the Trans-Canada Highway, drive past the day-use area and park near the small welcome centre. It is here that you purchase passes for camping or day hiking. The well-marked trailhead is just beyond the welcome centre, and in fact all of the hikes in this vicinity are identified by an abundance of bulletin boards, maps and markers. After buying a day pass,

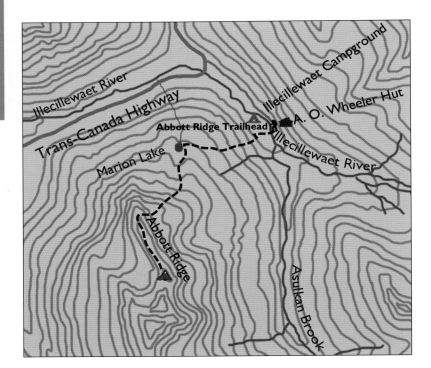

continue along the main road, and when it turns to gravel, follow the right fork to the remains of Glacier House.

The historic route through the remnants of Glacier House splits into two paths right away and surrounds the old foundation. This is an ugly, disheartening sight of what once was such a proud, grand structure. Follow the path that takes you around the right side to meet up with the trailhead.

The trailhead sign discloses that it is 4.9 km to the ridge. Other than relentless switchbacks through a stunning green forest, there really is not much to describe. The path is well worn, but the forest is not, as views through the thick growth are sporadic at best. An hour of clambering uphill approaches a fork in the trail, and a pleasant little lake, Marion, is a nice surprise for a break. At 1707 m high, the route has gained 481 m of the 1106 m required to summit. A quick diversion along the right-hand fork leads to a viewpoint overlooking the entrance to Connaught Tunnel.

Close inspection and patience will reveal train traffic entering and exiting the tunnel.

Continue into the forest and climb again, until the path leaves the trees and opens to a boulder patch and a magnificent alpine meadow. Now the hike is well worth the effort. The grind of uphill trekking always pays dividends; otherwise we would not put ourselves through it. The scenery is stunning and the pleasure of strutting through the alpine is exhilarating, yet calming.

Watch closely for a sign saying SHORTCUT and go that way. Eventually the trail passes by the Abbott Observatory, which is used to measure snowpack and other weather phenomena in the area. The route carries on past the observatory, winding up to the summit ridge. The ridge is extensive and becomes narrower as it progresses, so get in touch with your comfort zone before going beyond it. We came across a couple of worn resting areas with small cairns where scramblers had gone as far as they felt happy with.

Mount Bonney and its glacier are visible 5 km to the southwest, while the Hermit Range is unmistakable directly north. The amazing Sir Donald Range commands the eastern horizon.

Abbott history

This magnificent ridge, as well as Mount Abbott, Abbott Creek, Abbott Lake (in the Cariboo region), Abbott Peak, Abbott Street (in Vancouver) and the city of Abbotsford, BC, were all named after Harry Braithwaite Abbott. From 1884 to 1886, Abbott was superintendent of the CPR's western division, just two years after entering the service of the railway as a protégé of William Van Horne himself. From 1886 to 1897, during the early formation of Glacier House, Abbott was superintendent of the Pacific division.

Abbott was born in Abbotsford, Quebec, in 1829 and subsequently attended Montreal High School, followed by a further education at McGill College. After graduation, he applied his education as a civil engineer with a variety of railways, including the St. Lawrence & Atlantic, the Carillon & Grenville, the Brockville & Ottawa, the Eastern Extension, the Baltimore & Ohio and the Canada Central, finally making a long-lasting career with the CPR.

Abbott was stationed in Vancouver and resided there for most of his career, subsequently having the village of Abbotsford named in his honour, although one of the "t's" was dropped when the village was named by its owner, Charles Maclure. In 1909, Abbott purchased the Farr and Marpole ranches. The previous owner of the Marpole, Dalton P. Marpole, perished in a barn fire on this property in 1908. Dalton was the son of Richard Marpole, who would eventually assume Abbott's position as general superintendent of the Pacific division of the CPR. Abbott renamed the Farr and Marpole properties "Quincharden Ranch," and although he did not live at the ranch, he spent substantial time there. Abbott's son, Harry Hamilton Abbott, and his wife, Elizabeth, managed the ranch in his absence.

Abbott's brother, Sir John Abbott, was Prime Minister of Canada for 17 months following the death of Sir John A. Macdonald in 1891.

Mount Abbott, in the nearby vicinity of Abbott Ridge, received its name in 1886, and it is assumed the ridge was given its name around the same time. The ridge was not traversed until much later, by Alexander A. McCoubrey and his party in 1911. McCoubrey had moved to Canada from Scotland in 1900 at the age of 15, and four years later he was employed with the CPR in Manitoba. He was involved with initiating the sport of backcountry skiing in Manitoba and was instrumental in the formation of the Alpine Club of Canada (ACC) in 1906. His busy, inquisitive lifestyle encouraged him to take on responsibilities with the ACC as president from 1932 to 1934 and as both editor of the *Canadian Alpine Journal* and chairman of the Manitoba section of the ACC from 1931 to 1941. Most of McCoubrey's climbing and exploring took place in the breathtaking beauty of the Purcell Mountains, and he was responsible for many first ascents, including the Leaning Towers.

Marion Lake is an enchanting spot to rest before
pushing on to the final leg of Abbott Ridge.

A rare opening in the forest permits a glance across
the Asulkan Valley.

123

2. AVALANCHE CREST TRAIL

The alpine is utterly spectacular. Starting in thick forest that gradually thins, almost unnoticed, then progressing to a subalpine zone of stunted, leaner trees, and finally reaching the alpine above the treeline is an absolutely superb undertaking. I love it. The exertion is countered by the sheer sensation of the alpine. There is nothing quite as exquisite as walking past the last tree of the line and feeling the natural world changing around you. The temperature, humidity, sounds and smells all seem strikingly different from the trailhead several hundred metres below.

DIFFICULTY ▲ ▲

ELEVATION GAIN: END OF TRAIL: 850 M
                   RIDGE: 598 M

Trailhead: GPS: N51 15 58.9 W117 29 48.3
                                    Elevation: 1226 m

Avalanche Crest Trail End Point: GPS: N51 16 17.9 W117 28 28.5
                                    Elevation: 2076 m

Avalanche Crest Ridge: GPS: N51 16 16.9 W117 28 30.5
                                    Elevation: 2121 m

Trailhead: Drive the Trans-Canada Highway 3 km east of the Rogers Pass Centre to Illecillewaet Campground. Turn left to enter the campground area. Once on the paved campground road, drive past the campground on your right to the day parking area. There is a small welcome centre, where you must pay a fee for camping or for a day pass – truly a small price for such superb recreational value. After you have parked and paid, follow the paved road to its transition into a short gravel road. The trail marker is straight ahead.

As soon as your feet hit the path, the marker sends you in the correct direction. Take the left fork, as the right-hand one will take you to Perley Rock and the Sir Donald Trail. Just past this fork, the route begins a

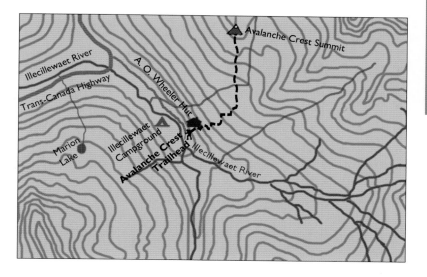

moderate ascent amid an old-growth forest. Within 5 to 10 minutes, you'll pass the first indicators of a ferocious windstorm in 2009 that caused several significant blowdowns, closing the Avalanche Trail for many weeks. A few minutes past the blown down area, the gradient increases significantly for a stretch of about 5 to 10 minutes, giving a good start to the day.

As the grade becomes a bit more tolerable, you'll encounter additional large, superb trees, now fractured and uprooted, enabling views across the Illecillewaet Valley that used to be hidden. The modest climb persists up to a small 1-km marker just on the edge of the right side of the path. It took me 28 minutes to reel in this first kilometre, which may give you an indication of the degree of the overall incline of this trail. My average time, with a scrambling pack and over level ground, is 12 minutes per kilometre, or a speed of 5 km/h.

The path now becomes noticeably friendlier. From here on up, the pitch decreases as the trail curves and turns leisurely upward for the next half-hour, with long level stretches that make the climb much more tolerable. At the one-hour mark, the path flattens completely for about 100 m as it roams over a stone walkway, washboards made of logs over bogs, and a small bridge over a stream. The elevation here is 1743 m above sea level, or a gain of about 500 m since the trailhead, with 300 m still to climb to the marked end of the trail. The trees begin to break here, presenting sensational views of the crest up to your right. A path marked VIEWPOINT darts off to the left just ten minutes before this.

Beyond the bridge, the path becomes quite narrow and gnarly with rocks, roots and running water for the balance of the journey. It is really nasty, so watch your step. Of course, the path continues upward, but soon the rewards become apparent. The forest is thinning, trees are becoming stunted and the sky appears larger. Loftier views of rivers, valleys and peaks become more frequent the higher you go.

Stepping ever upward becomes easier when you feel a couple of rock staircases beneath your feet about a half-hour into the trek. Vistas of scree slopes, ridges and open alpine will expose themselves as the remaining 100 m of elevation are conquered. The path enters the alpine into a wide, gaping gully that will astound you. Take your time to attain the last stretch of elevation through this trekker's wonderland. It is simply brilliant.

The trail's end is 2076 m high, but the truly amazing sites are 45 m higher, beyond the viewpoint marker. Take the extra five minutes to climb this stout slope on the north side of the valley to a lofty ridge. Once you are up on the crest, enjoy a magnificent, easygoing ridge walk that gradually ascends as far as you really want to take it.

From the ridge there is so much more to see, as there is a clear line of sight straight up and down Rogers Pass, looking north and west. The Illecillewaet Valley, the Hermit Range, the Illecillewaet Névé and Asulkan Brook are only a few of the magnificent treats that are waiting for you. Eagle Peak protrudes from the western horizon, and the peak of Avalanche Mountain stands 2 km to the northwest.

Avalanche Crest history

Avalanche Crest and Avalanche Mountain derive their names from obvious origins. Major Albert Bowman Rogers imparted the name after his party of Shuswap Indians were caught on the west side of the mountain in a snowslide that fell from the appropriately named crest. Rogers made the first ascent of the mountain, in 1881, but his party were not the only ones to share in the wrath of the mountain's namesake. Two reported encounters with avalanches from the crest include a group in 1908 led by Edward Wheeler, son of A.O. Wheeler, and an ensuing, unnamed ACC party.

Avalanches became such a paramount problem for the CPR that they eventually constructed over a mile of snowsheds below the mountain and crest. Snowfall in Rogers Pass at the time reached staggering depths of up to 12 m. This created a significant challenge for the engineers who designed the route. After all the hard work of getting the rails over the pass, they still had this seemingly insurmountable problem to deal with. The line was closed during the first winter after completion in 1885 to observe the activity and nature of the snowfall and subsequent avalanches. William Van Horne agreed to a massive system of 31 snow sheds, which reached a combined length of 6.5 km.

Avalanches all through the Pass closed the line repeatedly during the ensuing winters and springs, making travel and shipping unreliable, time-consuming and dangerous. Workers and engineers attempted to keep pace using locomotive rotary snowplows and pusher engines as well as brute physical labour with shovels, but regardless, there still remained the ongoing fight against the ceaseless snow.

As the battle continued, trains constantly derailed, lives were lost and repairs and maintenance were continual and expensive. An enormous avalanche on March 4, 1910, killed 58 workers who were clearing the line from a previous slide, thus cementing the decision by the CPR to finally surrender to Rogers Pass and go underground. For the ensuing seven years, the company focused its efforts on building the 9-km Connaught Tunnel, bypassing most of the treacherous avalanches and deep, heavy snow. Unfortunately, this would signal the eventual demise of Glacier House ten years later.

The Illecillewaet River leaves its headwaters and parallels the Trans-Canada Highway on its way to Upper Arrow Lake. I cannot express how amazing it is to be so high up in the mountains.

This hoary marmot blended with its environment so well that we were almost on top of it before we saw it. I'm certain he saw us long before we came upon him.

3. GREAT GLACIER TRAIL

Although you'll come to a sign claiming to mark the end of this trail, there is much more to explore beyond here. A daylong loop of experience awaits if you venture beyond the trailhead, as a wide open limestone expanse lies in front of you. Step off the path, head upward in a northerly direction and continue on glacier-scraped rock that was once covered in massive sheets of solid ice. The destruction left behind is immense and wondrous, and distracts you enough so that you scarcely notice the gain in elevation.

DIFFICULTY ▲

ELEVATION GAIN: 335 M TO END OF TRAIL
                    972 M TO GLACIER CREST SUMMIT

Trailhead: GPS: N51 15 58.9 W117 29 48.3
                                        Elevation: 1226 m

Great Glacier Summit: GPS: N51 14 59.2 W117 28 10.5
                                        Elevation: 1561 m

Extended version to Glacier Crest Summit: GPS: N51 14 21.3 W117 27 59.4
                                        Elevation: 2198 m

Trailhead: The trailhead for the Great Glacier route is situated among many others in a scrambler's paradise. The point of origin for all of these routes is at Illecillewaet Campground, 3 km west of the Rogers Pass Centre on the Trans-Canada Highway. Purchase your day pass at the small welcome centre and walk to where the pavement meets gravel. Watch for detailed signage that will guide you to the historic ruins of Glacier House.

From Illecillewaet Campground, follow the markers to the trailhead. The route passes through a clearing that contains the remains of Glacier House as it makes its way into the thick green forest. Five minutes in, the path splits, with signage sending you to the right-hand fork (straight). Another five minutes and a sign steers you left. The well-worn path cuts

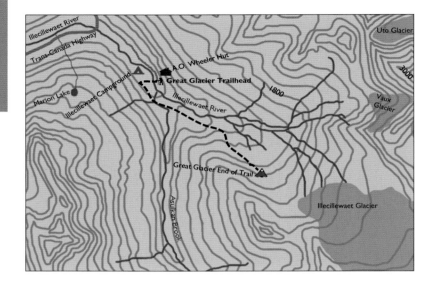

through this gorgeous, cool forest of western cedar, hemlock and under-growth of ferns and moss, alongside the Illecillewaet River. During the notorious forest fire season of 2003, we hiked this valley with temperatures outside the forest at an intolerable 36° C, while inside, it was a comfortable and cool 29°.

Another kilometre of strolling is interrupted by some moderate switchbacks that leave the forest and ascend the southwest slope of the Illecillewaet Valley. Tremendous views of Perley Rock and Mount Sir Donald and the amazing waterfalls of the northeast slope of the valley are nothing like you have ever seen before. There is so much water tumbling from these peaks that you wonder how it could possibly continue to fall in such volume all day and all night without stopping.

The path adheres to the hillside, climbing continually upward, passing two small weather-monitoring stations within a kilometre of each other. From the second of these weather stations, another kilometre of uphill strolling brings you to the official, signed end of the route. Cool glacial water runs freely down a rocky slope just beyond the trail's end.

Beyond here, travel the massive, open rock slabs left behind by the Great (Illecillewaet) Glacier, and venture to its toe. This open region, and the ensuing route, has but one faint track that fades at a large cairn 400 m up the path. This trail is not on any maps. Elevation gained from the end-of-trail marker to the cairns is 139 m. To reach the toe of the glacier, continue, without the aid of trails, another 800 m of distance with an elevation gain of 290 m. To complete this outstanding uncharted journey, work your way up the right (west) side of the ridge to the Glacier Crest summit (N51 14 20.8 W117 28 02.7). The top of the Glacier Crest Trail is an additional 185 m upward.

This spectacular view across the Illecillewaet Valley from the Great Glacier trail reveals the lower stretch, and most of the switchbacks, of the Perley Rock and Mount Sir Donald trails. The eastern headwaters of the Illecillewaet River are evident as winter runoff cascades toward the valley floor.

4. GLACIER CREST TRAIL

Most of this scramble consists of a steady uphill climb through a marvellous, humid forest. The persistent climb gives way, though, to a truly incredible view of glacier, water, rock and snow. Very few places on earth allow us to become spectators to a display such as the formation of a river at its headwaters. Here, with some effort, we are able to observe massive amounts of water tumble downward from several tables of solid ice to converge, as though by instinct, into a single, solid river. From the upper reaches of the trail, the stages of glacial origins to multiple feeder streams to the end product of a mighty river can all be seen with a simple shifting of the eyes.

DIFFICULTY ▲ ▲ ▲
ELEVATION GAIN: 9722 M

Trailhead:	GPS: N51 15 58.9 W117 29 48.3
	Elevation: 1226 m
Glacier Crest Summit:	GPS: N51 14 21.3 W117 27 59.4
	Elevation: 2198 m

Trailhead: This and many other trailheads are situated in the Illecillewaet recreation region, just 3 km west of the Rogers Pass Centre on the Trans-Canada Highway. The area is signed on the highway as Illecillewaet Campground. Relative to other Rocky Mountain parks, this region is unknown.

The Illecillewaet recreational region consists of at least seven treks, two magnificent valleys, glaciers, streams, rivers, waterfalls, a mountain cabin, tarns, meadows, mountains, ridges, an Alpine Club of Canada hut, and historic ruins. If you wish to stay a couple of nights, there is a wonderful campground.

Before you begin, there seems to be a bit of an elevation conflict that you must be aware of. At the trailhead, Parks Canada states that the summit of the Glacier Crest Trail is 2045 m, and their website makes the same

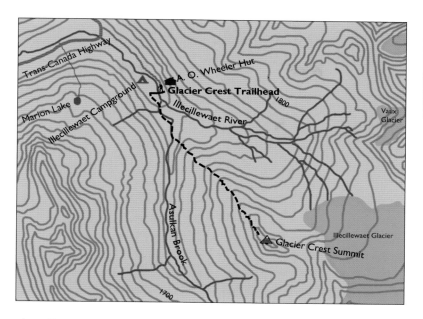

claim. It also says that the "elevation of crest" is at 2255 m. My GPS readings place the lengthy boulder field below the summit ridge at 2064 m and the summit arête at 2198 m. Whatever the case, I urge you to go the distance to achieve the true high point. The sight as you survey two distinct, beautiful valleys with just a turn of your head is unequivocally extraordinary.

From Illecillewaet Campground's day parking lot, follow the markers to the trailhead. As the route makes its way into a thick, green, old-growth forest, it passes through a clearing that contains the remains of Glacier House. Five minutes in, the path splits, with signage sending you to the right (straight). Five minutes later another sign steers you to the right again.

There is a slight incline in the forest that quickly settles into a wide, flat path for about 500 m. A high bridge rises above Asulkan Brook, which marks the 1.2-km point of the trek. The hike pushes upward from the brook, and within a couple of short minutes a fork in the trail is accompanied by a sign pointing you to the left, marking 3.5 km remaining on this hike.

The next hour and a half or so is a climb of switchbacks through an increasingly thinning forest that allows the occasional view of Abbott Ridge, Mount Abbott and the Asulkan Ridge. The trail is surrounded by a variety of ferns, mosses, liverworts and broad-leafed shrubs. During the seemingly endless switchbacks, watch for the distinctive western hemlock with curved trunks. Because of the steep slope (causing a phenomenon called soil creep) and an impenetrable forest canopy, some of these magnificent trees begin life by careening out of the side of a bank on an angle, only to right themselves years later, creating a unique curved trunk near their base.

The grade continues, unrelenting in releasing progressively more astounding beauty as you move higher and higher. The forest progresses through the evolution to alpine within a short span of 150 to 200 m of elevation. The change is quite abrupt, and soon you are wandering over a boulder field that seems endless. This, however, is not the final destination. All sights in a 270° west, north and south arc are included in this stunning panorama, but the best is only another 134 m higher.

The view from the crest is magnificent. Lookout Mountain is 1.3 km to the southeast, while Young Peak is 4.1 km southward. The Asulkan Valley and Glacier are below almost directly south. Looking across the Illecillewaet Valley, you can easily spot Mount Sir Donald and Perley Rock along with the toe of Great Glacier. Breathtaking.

If you are feeling adventurous, continue down to the rocky exposure of the Illecillewaet Valley and proceed to the toe of the glacier. I would not recommend hiking on the glacier, though, unless you are properly equipped and knowledgeable. The unmarked, tailless region will gradually take you to the end of the Great Glacier Trail, allowing a complete, all-encompassing loop of these two marvellous routes.

Glacier Crest history

This ridge earned its name from members of the Appalachian Mountain Club in 1895. Glacier Crest is just that, a crest between the Asulkan and Illecillewaet Glaciers, providing spectacular views of both, with the Illecillewaet Glacier to the east and the Asulkan Glacier to the west. This sharp, narrow ridge was carved by glaciers that flowed down both sides of the ridge.

The view across the Asulkan Valley from the
Glacier Crest trail is immense.

5. PERLEY ROCK

From this dazzling spot in Glacier National Park, the foremost standout without a doubt is Illecillewaet Névé. The southern and southeastern views are dominated by this massive sheet of compressed ice. You may now have some comprehension of why there can be so much water flowing and falling into the valleys around here. An ice axe or a hiking pole is recommended for a lengthy snow slope at the final phase of the trek.

DIFFICULTY ▲ ▲ ▲ ▲
ELEVATION GAIN: 1181 M

Trailhead:	GPS: N51 15 58.9 W117 29 48.3
	Elevation: 1226 m
Perley Rock Peak Summit:	GPS: N51 14 56.5 W117 26 32.6
	Elevation: 2407 m

Trailhead: The GPS coordinates, as with all trailheads in the Illecillewaet outdoor neighbourhood, begin at the Glacier Park Welcome Centre.

The route takes an immediate right turn down to the near shore of the Illecillewaet River. Beneath the canopy of a thick forest of hemlock, spruce and cedars, the path widens and has the feel of being significantly well travelled. Ferns and mosses are rare standouts within the dense, green woods.

The first signed fork in the trail occurs six to seven minutes into the walk, directing you to stay straight. Here, the hike begins to climb and the tree trunks become noticeably thicker, fatter. You'll cross a feeder stream just before the 1-km mark. Shortly into this magnificent forest, the path opens up into an equally magnificent valley. A 30- to 40-minute walk through this area gives unprecedented views of Mount Sir Donald, Terminal Peak and Uto Peak to the east and Lookout Mountain straight ahead to the south. The valley bottom trail ducks in and out of groves of trees, sometimes briefly obscuring the view, but more often than not you become transfixed by views of the beauty of the Illecillewaet Valley.

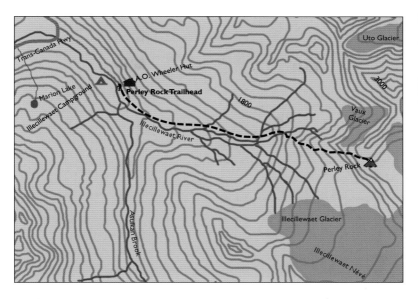

As the hike creeps slowly upward, the spray from glacier melt will cool and refresh you before you press on up the switchbacks that linger just a few short minutes away. Water from Vaux Glacier tumbles down from above without any consideration for what lies in its path. It travels unrestrained over rock and vegetation as if running scared from something hidden above. The trail crosses two aluminum bridges five minutes apart. The first one dips down into a gorge that puts you just a few feet over a violent, yet calming, Vaux Creek. Stand and let the spray wet your face. So much water.

After you've crossed the second bridge, all that is left are switchbacks. However, the higher you go, the more incredible the scenery becomes. Mountain peaks and ranges that cradle glaciers surround the valley they feed. Below, small glacier ponds and the scrape marks left behind by the receding glaciers become evident as the path winds upward. Some 15 to 20 minutes more and the trail will reach a fork where the routes are clearly marked. Sir Donald Trail carries on to the left, Perley Rock to the right. Take the right branch and activate your climbing legs once more.

The path from the junction begins as steep switchbacks through a thin forest of spruce and fir. This persistent uphill grunt takes you beyond the trees when the route leaves the forest for the alpine. Open talus slopes become part of the landscape as the upward grind continues. Finally, an impressive snow slope sits directly in your path and the ledge of Perley Rock seems within your grasp. The snow can be intimidating, and I have seen hikers clamber way down to the base of it, only to climb all the way back up on the opposite side. This is quite understandable because one slip at the top of the snow slope will send you sliding downward, out of control, possibly all the way to the bottom. And where the snow ends, the rocks take over. So be careful. An ice axe or hiking staff comes in handy here for balance.

Beyond the snow slope, cairns mark the way through rocks and small boulders. It will require one last burst of energy to scramble to the wide base of the enormous rock outcropping known as Perley Rock.

Everything seen from this chunk of the planet is, quite frankly, just big. Illecillewaet Névé, Mount Sir Donald, Lookout Mountain, the Illecillewaet Valley, even the sky – all are enormous. Everywhere you look the beauty is immense.

Perley Rock history

Glacier House, Mount Stephen House at Field and Fraser Canyon House at North Bend, BC, were all constructed to accommodate tourists along the CPR route. These three facilities were built out of necessity rather than choice, as these locations created substantial hardship for locomotives hauling dining cars and sleeping cars up and down the steep grades.

Perley Rock is named after Harry Allison Perley, the first manager of Glacier House before it became a popular CPR stop. After railway construction was completed, there was still an abundance of work to do on snowsheds, stations, yards, terminals and the organization of schedules and operations. All this effort was going to take significant time to complete, but the railway was already transporting travellers. To accommodate these early passengers, CPR manager William Van Horne and H.A. Perley signed a contract on October 26, 1887, to have Perley operate Glacier House.

The contract was somewhat distinctive in that it allowed Perley to manage the place for his own benefit and take the profits for himself:

"… the Company to make no charge for the use of the house and premises, and the said Perley to have the receipts from the Hotel and Lunch Rooms, as sole remuneration for keeping the same…" The company was also to provide transportation for Perley, his wife and staff to and from Glacier House. Another benefit of the contract was that the CPR was to supply and ship fuel for the winter months.

In return for these and many other perks, Perley agreed to maintain the furniture and fixtures and return them to the CPR in good condition at the expiry of the contract. Additionally, he was expected to manage operations according to the CPR's taste: "Perley to manage the Hotel in such a way as to give entire satisfaction to the Company…" He was also to ensure that guests were comfortable and happy: "… and shall employ a first-class cook and competent waiters who shall be kept neat and clean as to dress and otherwise; and who shall be civil and attentive to the guests … and so as to give entire satisfaction to the travelling public…"

Perley certainly surpassed his side of the bargain and was hailed by many as being a most hospitable manager. He added many personal touches to the interior and exterior of Glacier House, producing an exquisite luxury hotel in the wilderness that was used as a base for mountaineering, exploring and relaxing. There was no other place like it in all of North America.

As the manager of Glacier House for somewhere between eight and ten years, Perley escorted and directed many guests into the surrounding mountains and glaciers. One of his favourite spots for easy access and remarkable viewing would be named Perley Rock.

From Perley Rock the vastness of the Illecillewaet Névé will stop you in your tracks.

Mount Sir Donald rises high above anything else in this
dazzling region of British Columbia.

The peak of Mount Sir Donald seen from the trail to
Perley Rock and Mount Sir Donald. There is so much water
through the valleys in this park, it is difficult to grasp.

140

6. SIR DONALD TRAIL

This trek is a beautiful walk through a vivid green forest and a magnificent open valley surrounded by a wealth of ceaseless waterfalls and streams. It is a shame that it is interrupted by a very steep climb. Used mainly as a base camp for summiting Mount Sir Donald, the col between Uto Peak and Mount Sir Donald may be populated with tents and climbers, but I am certain they will not mind sharing the view.

DIFFICULTY ▲ ▲ ▲
ELEVATION GAIN: 940 M

Trailhead:	GPS: N51 15 58.9 W117 29 48.3
	Elevation: 1226 m
Sir Donald Trail Summit:	GPS: N51 15 32.4 W117 26 40.8
	Elevation: 2166 m

Trailhead: The trailhead is located in the Illecillewaet Campground recreation area, 3 km west of the summit of Rogers Pass. This minor exit off the highway is a busy little mecca for campers, hikers, scramblers, climbers, cross-country skiers and picnickers. Enter the campground off the east side of the Trans-Canada Highway, drive past the day-use area and park in the lot just past the small welcome centre, where you can purchase passes for camping or day hiking. The well-marked trailhead lies just beyond the welcome centre. In fact, all of the routes in this vicinity are identified by an abundance of bulletin boards, maps and markers. From the welcome centre, walk up the road as it turns to gravel, and the sign to the trailhead will appear in front of you. The A.O. Wheeler Alpine Club of Canada hut is nestled among the trees to your left.

A quick right turn down to the eastern bank of the Illecillewaet River initiates the trek to the summit of the Sir Donald Trail. The leisurely stroll is highlighted by the different textures of green within the protection of the forest. The path is wide and well travelled for the most part, permitting

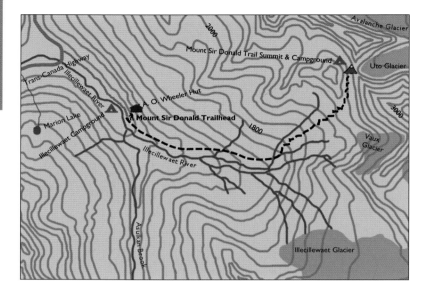

easy gazing at the surrounding ferns and mosses that dominate the thick underbelly of the spruce, hemlock and cedars.

About six to seven minutes into the walk, you'll come to the first fork, where a sign directs you to stay straight. The trail begins to climb and the forest becomes thicker. You'll cross a feeder stream just before reaching the 1-km mark.

Five to six minutes of walking this magnificent forest sees it open up into an equally magnificent valley. This is fantastic. The long walk through this area gives unparalleled views of Mount Sir Donald, Terminal Peak and Uto Peak to the east and Lookout Mountain straight ahead to the south. For 30 to 40 minutes, the trail darts in and out of sections of forest of varying length, but for the most part the path sorts its way upward in the wide open Illecillewaet Valley.

Mingling with the sweat of your efforts as the hike begins to ascend is spray from the torrent of meltwater tumbling to the rocks below. The Vaux Glacier releases its payload at such an incredible rate that it is difficult to comprehend the amount of ice and snow that must be present in one spot to sustain such a massive flow of water. As you approach the first of two aluminum bridges, the trail dips down into a gorge that puts you just a few feet above a violently churning yet somehow calming Vaux Creek. Stand a moment and feel the spray on your face. Such a lot of water.

Switchbacks become steeper after the second bridge despite the spacious, flat, uniform appearance of this wonderful valley. As the route ascends, the scenery improves, and the site of mountain peaks, glaciers, tarns, streams and waterfalls should satisfy all of your fantasies of natural beauty. Look closely for scrapings on the limestone tables left behind by receding glaciers. About 15 to 20 minutes farther upward, the trail reaches a clearly marked fork. Sir Donald Trail carries on to the left, the Perley Rock route to the right.

Watch your step along here, as the path takes off along the bottom of a wide gully and loose rocks can easily roll even the strongest ankles. More beauty is revealed to you as a reward for climbing higher. Almost as rewarding is an enjoyably level patch of ground to rest before the final push. The trek now finishes with a quick spurt of 153 m of elevation gain, partially along the Vaux Glacier moraine, to the top of a wide open basin. Above you to the northeast looms the unmistakable tower of Mount Sir Donald, with the Vaux Glacier in the foreground.

The col you will land on is used as a base camp for climbing the spectacular Mount Sir Donald. To the southwest, 9.5 km away, stands Mount Bonney. The Illecillewaet Glacier is to the south and Uto Peak is directly north.

Mount Sir Donald history

On November 7, 1885, the last railway spike linking the east and the west ends of the Canadian Pacific Railway was driven into the ground at Craigellachie, BC, by a director of the CPR, Sir Donald Alexander Smith. The ceremony was small and brief compared with other such commemorative events, and there was very little fanfare. Had the Governor General, Lord Lansdowne, been able to attend as initially planned, the event might have been more of a spectacle, but he was required to return to Ottawa just before the ceremony, despite having made the long trip out West for the event. Lord Lansdowne had even had a silver spike manufactured to commemorate the moment, a distinctive touch compared to the gold spike that completed the first US transcontinental route with the connection of the Central Pacific and Union Pacific railroads in 1869. As it turned out, though, the silver spike was unavailable, so William Van Horne declared, "The last spike will be just as good an iron one as there is between Montreal and Vancouver..."

It is that same Sir Donald Alexander Smith that Mount Sir Donald was named for by way of a federal order-in-council, meaning the name was decided by Cabinet and then officially endorsed by the Governor General. In addition to being a director of the CPR, Smith was a Hudson's Bay Co. officer as well as a politician, diplomat and philanthropist. The mountain had originally been named "Syndicate Peak" as a tribute to all the principal financiers of the CPR.

Although it was named in 1885, the mountain was not climbed until five years later, by Emil Huber, Carl Sulzer and their porter, Harry Cooper. Huber and Sulzer, both amateur Swiss mountaineers, arrived at Glacier House on July 21, 1890, with the ambition of nothing short of summiting Mount Sir Donald during that climbing season. The allure of Mount Sir Donald was twofold: it was, and still is, technically challenging; and it has a distinctive Matterhorn-like shape. The party completed their goal just five days after their arrival, ascending Mount Sir Donald via the southwest wall on July 26.

The pair had climbed to the top of nearby Uto Peak on July 23 to gain a vantage of Sir Donald, and it was there that they devised what appeared to be the easiest way to the summit of Mount Sir Donald. Their course from Uto Peak to Mount Sir Donald across the edge of the Vaux Glacier is the most noted route still taken today.

On the Mount Sir Donald trail switchbacks, this resting spot gives up a spectacular vista of the Illecillewaet Valley looking west.

7. THE HERMIT

The Hermit is a remarkable scramble to an equally remarkable destination. A dense forest at the outset and a stairway of rock at the top are but a couple of the exceptional highlights of the Hermit Trail. Although the route is classed as a scramble because of its uncompromising climb, camping is permitted in the meadow. The summit of the Hermit does not lie on the top of a mountain but is an oasis of horizontal ground along the side of the Hermit Range.

DIFFICULTY ▲ ▲ ▲ ▲
ELEVATION GAIN: 810 M

Trailhead: GPS: N51 18 50.0 W117 30 45.7
                              Elevation: 1296 m

Hermit Meadows Campground: GPS: N51 19 46.2 W117 31 49.7
                              Elevation: 2106 m

Trailhead: From the Rogers Pass Centre, drive east for 1 km, looking for the signed parking lot for the Hermit Trail on the north (left) side of the Trans-Canada Highway.

The trail leaves the highway behind for a dark, thick, old-growth forest. The journey begins its steep, persistent climb on a root-grown path almost immediately. The route gets redirected just a few short minutes into the forest, where a sign sends you to the right and informs you that the Hermit Meadows are 2.8 km away. Within that distance you'll accomplish 810 m of elevation gain. A steep grade indeed.

Enjoy this upward trek, because within 15 minutes it becomes still more intense. Some 45 minutes from the trailhead the drudgery of the steep climb is broken when the forest opens and presents magnificent scenery of the Selkirk Mountains and the Sir Donald Range to the southeast and south respectively. Mount Tupper can be clearly seen due east. By this point, you've accomplished almost half of the total elevation gain.

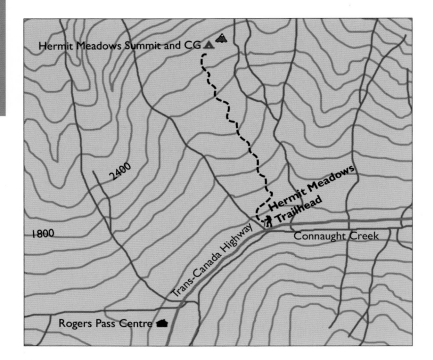

The grade tends to ease now as it works its way up over solid rock and through open air. The route gradually makes its way up to a subalpine forest of stunted trees, and another 20 minutes from where the path broke out of the forest, look for a viewpoint on the left. This is a great spot for a bit of a rest; it is open and the horizon directly across Rogers Pass is filled with the mammoth sight of Mount Macdonald. This is just such a great way to spend a day.

Fifteen minutes up from the lookout, the trail becomes a structure of stone steps and bridges. Someone with, I presume, incredible strength and talent has committed much time and effort to design and manufacture such a wonderful creation. Flat, hard stones have been moved into place to produce a stairway upward through the alpine, crossing streams and small fissures, and they are solid and unyielding. At the first stepping stone, there is 140 m of elevation gain remaining.

Some 15 minutes later and 80 m up, you'll come upon a rope anchored in stone, likely set by the same people who built the stairway. The rope seems to be more practical on the way back down, to help navigate some awkward stones. Although it is only a few metres long, it proves to be very useful. More flat rock stairs and a short, narrow ravine bring an end to this incredible journey.

Exposed rock, moraines, a creek and meadows greet you at the top of the stairs. The wide open Hermit Meadows present views of the Selkirk Range, with Mount Macdonald in the forefront. Amazing.

Looking west, Rogers Pass as seen from The Hermit summit and campground. This is truly breathtaking.

The Hermit campground and summit. Glacier National
Park. Bear boxes in the foreground with the Hermit
Range as the backdrop.

This view of Mount Macdonald is one of many
incredible sights from The Hermit summit.

148

8. COPPERSTAIN MOUNTAIN

This is a short, easy scramble from Copperstain Pass Campground, but it will be a long, arduous jaunt if you combine trips to both the pass and the summit into only one day. The scramble itself is the easiest and shortest climb in this guide. It offers zero exposure, a well-worn path, minimal scree, and it is actually not very steep. It is truly that easy. The payoff, though, is magnificent.

DIFFICULTY ▲
ELEVATION GAIN: 525 M

Trailhead:	Copperstain Pass Campground:	GPS: N51 21 43.8 W117 25 47.9
		Elevation: 2088 m
Copperstain Mountain Summit:		GPS: N51 17 00.5 W117 17 15.7
		Elevation: 2613 m

Trailhead: The trailhead originates from the beautiful Copperstain Pass Campground. To get here as the starting point, please refer to the chapter on this campground.

The stretch of 16 km from the Copperstain Pass trailhead near the highway has more than double the elevation gain, for a tally of 1738 m. Therefore, it is recommended as a two- to three-day combined backpacking/scrambling sojourn. With only 525 m of gain, this easy scramble is an extraordinary excursion from the campground.

The peak is unmistakable and ever present, as it is less than 2 km from the campground. From your campsite, after your morning coffee, simply walk through the woods toward the summit. Many faint trails are scattered through the forest, with all of them culminating in a single main path. This route will be picked up quickly. The base of the mountain is about 800 m from the campground, so enjoy the 10- to 15-minute stroll in the forest.

Gradually the woods thin, the ground inclines and you realize you are beginning your ascent. Soon enough the forest breaks and the earth

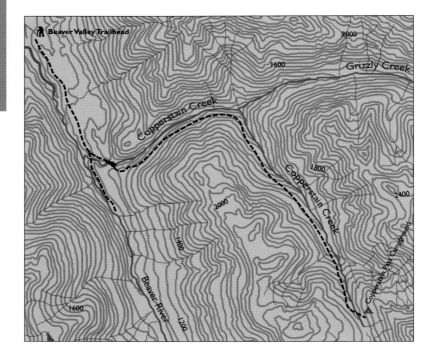

beneath your feet changes to a gentle talus slope. The path that takes you to the summit is well beaten and has negligible scree. Switchbacks are scarce and there is certainly no hand-over-hand scrambling. Lovely. This open, easygoing, enjoyable climb is merely an uphill walk on an open grade.

The summit arrives quite soon, and your summit sit-down may actually last longer than the ascent. The western sky presents the sharpened peaks of the Sir Donald Range, and can hold you up here for hours. The menacing peak of Mount Sir Donald is the real eyecatcher. It is the tall one directly to the west of you. Uto Peak rests on Sir Donald's north flank, and Terminal Peak resides to the south. This is the glacier laden "back" side of the Illecillewaet climbing area of Glacier National Park. Moonraker Peak stands on the distant eastern horizon, 4.5 km away.

Glacier House history

In 1871, the CPR hired a Scot, Sandford Fleming, to find a way around or through many obstacles to the success of a coast-to-coast railway. One of the three biggest challenges was to find a practicable route through the Rockies. The other two were the Laurentian Shield and the canyons of the Thompson and the Fraser rivers. Fleming became chief engineer of the CPR, as he had prior experience as chief engineer with the Intercontinental Railway.

Fleming initially recommended a route through Yellowhead Pass, but this choice was farther north than the CPR desired. The company's executive committee feared that US railways would penetrate over the international boundary into Canada if the CPR did not establish a southern route. The final choice cut through the Selkirk Mountains by way of Rogers Pass, even though the Yellowhead Pass was the superior route because it had substantially less elevation change and a longer grade.

Rogers Pass was discovered in 1881 by Major Albert Bowman Rogers. Rogers graduated from Yale University in 1853 and began work as an engineer on the Erie Canal and then with the Chicago, Milwaukee, St. Paul & Pacific Railroad, called the Milwaukee Road. In 1862, during the Civil War, he was a major in the US cavalry. His reputation with the Milwaukee Road earned him the nickname "The Railway Pathfinder," which came to the ear of a member of the executive committee of the CPR, James Jerome Hill. Hill hired Rogers in 1881 to command the CPR's mountain route-finding. Fleming was not directly involved with the appointment of Rogers, but he would oversee the new hire's work in 1883 and came to praise Rogers highly.

The first order of business for Rogers was to send out exploration parties to survey the Bow River and investigate Howse and Kicking Horse passes. Although early explorers firmly believed there was no workable route through the Selkirks, Rogers's stubbornness got the best of him and he took on the task himself. He and his party approached the pass from the west, departing from what is now Revelstoke, BC, in June of 1881 by way of the Illecillewaet River. The route was based on an 1866 report by Walter Moberly, a BC government engineer who had had one of his crew view the area from some of the mountains around the Illecillewaet Valley. Moberly insisted there was no pass.

Nonetheless, Rogers was confident that a pass did indeed exist, and from the vantage point of what today is called Mount Sir Donald he saw what he believed to be a workable route. However, the party exhausted their supplies before they could investigate the remaining 29 km of the pass, so they were forced to return the following season. This time, they approached from the east, up the Beaver River, and had to make two attempts, as they again ran out of provisions. Finally, on July 24, 1882, Major Rogers spotted the slope of Mount Sir Donald, the mountain he had climbed the previous summer, and the pass was henceforth known as Rogers Pass. Although he was paid a $5,000 bonus for discovering the pass, the only reward he had agreed to was that the pass be named after him. So he framed the $5,000 cheque and hung it on his wall rather than cash it. This created years of accounting problems for the CPR, and eventually the general manager, William Van Horne, offered Rogers a gold watch if he would just cash the cheque.

With the pass, of course, came the railway bringing tourists to the unexplored, virgin mountains. With most of the principal peaks in Europe already conquered, the summits of North America became a very appealing proposition to professional and amateur mountaineers alike. In 1888, the first recreational ascent of a mountain in North America was achieved by reverends William Spotswood Green and Henry Swanzy when they summited Mount Bonney. This marked Glacier National Park as the base for mountaineering fun in North America barely two years after the park's formation in 1886.

Once the rail line through to the Pacific was completed, it became obvious that the area of Great Glacier (Illecillewaet) was a uniquely beautiful part of the country. The CPR wasted no time in taking advantage of such magnificence, and by late 1886 had created a lodge of unparalleled elegance: Glacier House. Although Banff National Park obtained national-park status a year before Glacier and Yoho, Glacier House was a first in the Rockies. The Banff Springs Hotel did not open until two years later, and it was Glacier House that became the template for the Chateau Lake Louise.

The logic behind Glacier House was twofold. The CPR needed to have a dining car atop the long, steep climb out of the Rockies to the Selkirks. But dining cars were excruciatingly heavy, and even with specially designed locomotives, they still slowed the climb to the summit of Rogers Pass. To solve this problem, the railway erected a dining hall with a chalet and a few rooms at the base of Great Glacier, which became known as Glacier House. The facility was a great popular success, and it was expanded in 1892 and again in 1904. At its peak, the Great House featured 90 rooms, a billiard hall and a bowling alley. Soon after, a small village, Summit City, sprang up with saloons, hotels, a general store, a school and homes.

Eleven years after the ascent of Mount Bonney by Green and Swanzy, the CPR imported two Swiss guides, Edward Feuz and Christian Hasler, to Glacier House to help develop the region for climbing and assist guests in reaching the summits of these amazing peaks. The idea was to give the lodge's growing clientele not only a feeling of confidence and safety but also a sense of exotic adventure. By 1903, at least 40 peaks in the Glacier National Park region had been summited, and many of the trails cut by these Swiss guides over a century ago are still used by hikers and climbers today. The guides were a tremendous success and helped to realize Van Horne's dream of transforming a vast wilderness into a profitable, elegant playground for tourists.

The good times would last for a while, but impending danger has a way of taking the life out of a party sometimes. And so it was with Glacier House, as the unwavering onslaught of snowfall and avalanches caused the eventual demise of both the lodge itself and Summit City. With an average annual snowfall of 12 m at Rogers Pass, and the extreme gradient of the adjacent peaks, it was almost impossible to keep the rail line clear throughout most of the winter and spring. Too many deaths and too many derailments finally forced the CPR mainline under the pass. Van Horne made the decision to tunnel in 1910, and by 1917 the 9-km Connaught Tunnel was complete.

Glacier House continued to receive guests, but without the train pulling up and stopping in front of the grand hotel, most of the appeal was lost. Disembarking at the entrance to the tunnel and travelling the rest of the way by horse and buggy simply did not sit well with tourists. As visitors dwindled, so did Summit City, and in 1925 the hotel was closed for good. In 1929 the CPR did the unthinkable and demolished Glacier House. For fear of fire or collapse, either one causing potential liability, the railway executive decided that the safest end to Glacier House would be to simply take it down.

The next 40 years saw very few travellers. Even with the construction of the Alpine Club of Canada's A.O. Wheeler Hut in 1946, only a handful of people frequented this stunning landscape. With the completion of the Trans-Canada Highway through Rogers Pass in 1962, the beauty that had been paused, waiting for climbers to return, was finally reawakened once again for us to enjoy. So, drive up to the base of the mountains and the remaining foundations of the great Glacier House and look around in wondrous awe as you pass over the exact same paths that the trailbreakers built in the heyday of this amazing place.

9. MOUNT FIELD

Even though the bulk of the hike to this summit is reached through a thick forest of spruce and fir, the last 500 m of elevation gain finally opens wide to present astounding views. With about 62 m left before the summit, you'll encounter a rock wall that has only a couple of accessible, penetrable spots. There is a steep hand-over-fist climb here of only about 5 m, so keep this in mind before your departure. You may decide not to challenge this obstacle once you are up there.

DIFFICULTY ▲ ▲ ▲
ELEVATION GAIN: 1392 M

Trailhead:	GPS: N51 24 17.3 W116 28 58.7
	Elevation: 1254 m
Burgess Pass Summit:	GPS: N51 25 48.5 W116 29 08.1
	Elevation: 2204 m
Rockband:	GPS: N51 25 50.8 W116 27 51.5
	Elevation: 2584 m
Mount Field Summit:	GPS: N51 24 17.3 W116 28 58.7
	Elevation: 2646 m

The first 3.5 km of the trek to the summit of Mount Field takes the same route as Mount Burgess up to the point where the Mount Burgess hike veers off the main trail.

Trailhead: From the Yoho National Park Information Centre in Field, BC, head east on the Trans-Canada Highway for 1.4 km. Turn left (north) onto the only unpaved road and immediately make a left turn at the first fork. Keep left for 400 m and the Burgess Pass trailhead will greet you.

Within the first couple of minutes, you'll pass a rare find of natural springs on the right side of the trail. There seems to be two or three of

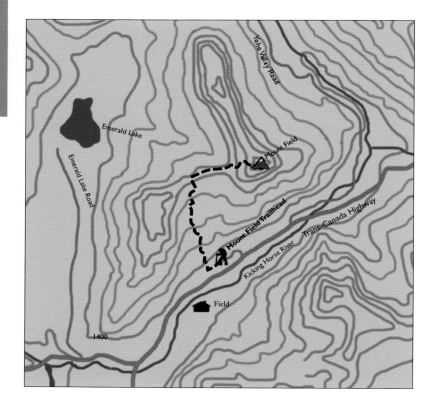

these underground aquifers spouting from the hillside and beneath rotting logs. A fork in the path lies just beyond them. Choose the right-hand route.

Within a forest of Engelmann spruce and lodgepole pine, there are occasional western red cedars that seem completely out of place. These sporadic trees are taller and thicker than the other evergreens and have distinctive grey, vertically lined bark.

About 500 m into the hike there is a short boardwalk of stairs consisting of about six long platforms. Although the boards are old, there is a distinct smell of damp, exposed wood when they are wet. This smell, combined with that of a few nearby western red cedars and a mossy forest floor, results in a unique scent unlike any other I have experienced in the Rockies.

The exquisite sound of a small stream resonates through the forest as the hike begins a mild uphill climb, and within 20 minutes from the trailhead this stream exposes itself on the right. The path then leaves the stream as it graduates to a much steeper ascent, with sharp switchbacks interspersed with long flat stretches. You'll cross this same stream again in another 20 minutes or so, and it is the last source of water for the entire climb. Stop here and top up your thirst and canisters.

As the trail winds upward beyond the stream, the forest opens and the view of Field and its rocky guardians becomes ever clearer. This scenery makes the ceaseless climbing tolerable. Another kilometre brings the path to a wide, dry avalanche trench. The power of tumbling snow is evident, as the underbrush and trees have been replaced by a broad swath of rock and rubble. To cross this debris field, follow cairns and a faint track. Once on the other side, follow the cairns up the avalanche slope until the path into the forest reappears on your right. Someone from Parks Canada has packed a chain saw up here to cut a convenient notch in a large fallen tree for us.

For another 45 minutes, the forest gradually thins and the trees become shorter as you reach the subalpine. Look for a tree on the right that has two distinct axe or hatchet wedges hacked from it. An additional 15 to 20 minutes past this tree, on the left side of the open hillside, is a faint path leading to the summit. There are piles of rocks on either side (GPS N51 24 56.0 W116 29 30.4; elevation 1783 m). From this spot, the faint track to the summit of Mount Burgess takes off to the left onto the exposed slope, toward an island of trees that is easily spotted.

Just beyond the Mount Burgess junction, the trail takes up a long section of switchbacks that weaves in and out of the forests. After 15 or 20 minutes of this, the path opens to traverse a disturbingly steep slope of shale. Crossing this slope delivers a fabulous view of the entire length of Emerald Lake, though, from Emerald Lake Lodge at the south (left) end to the lake's main feeder streams at the north end. The feeder streams come down from glaciers on the President Range, carrying debris and creating a wonderful alluvial fan at the northern end of Emerald Lake. This is just an amazing site. Stop and take it all in; don't be in a hurry.

Five or ten minutes later, you reach the summit of Burgess Pass, at 7.3 km from the trailhead. From the pass, follow the sign directing foot traffic to Yoho Pass and Yoho Lake. The next half-hour consists of an undulating, forested walk uphill, level and downhill again. There is even a set of wooden stairs. Eventually a large sign prevents you from entering the famous grounds of the Burgess Shale. The massive scree slope of Mount Field dominates the view to the right as the trail breaks from the forest and begins a large left-sweeping curve on its way to Yoho pass and lake.

Find your way onto the slope and begin slogging up the abundance of scree. As you head upward, bear to the far right (east) side of the slope. As mentioned in the introduction to this route, it is necessary to scramble over a rock wall as you near the summit, and by far the easiest – though not the only – route over this wall is through a notch at the far right end of it. But since the area directly beneath the wall is this steep slope of debris that has fallen from it, I strongly recommend that you aim for the notch now, from the base of the scree slope, rather than try to manoeuvre over to it after you come face-to-face with the wall. Traversing the scree diagonally in this way is also a bit easier than trying to go straight up it. There are only a few definitive faint trails on the slope, so just pick your way as you like.

Upon reaching the far end of the wall, look for the openings marked with cairns (I could only find two). Decide for yourself whether the rock climbing, although brief, is your forte or not. The sights from beneath the wall are just as fantastic as the ones from the summit.

Mount Field history

William Van Horne named this easily climbed mountain after Cyrus West Field in 1883. Van Horne was constantly raising money for his railway, and he had brought Field to the Selkirks to court him as a potential investor. Field declined. In hindsight, though, an investment in the CPR would have done well for him and perhaps offset some bad investment decisions he made late in his life which left him penniless.

Born in 1819 in Stockbridge, Massachusetts, Field was highly educated and had begun working in a textile house at the age of 15. He eventually became the principal in the business, amassing a huge fortune and retiring at the age of 34 in 1853. A few short months later, he was approached by the chief promoter of the Electric Telegraph Company to invest in a trans-Atlantic cable from St. John's, Nfld., to the Irish coast. After doing his due diligence, Field made the investment and convinced many other New York financiers to get aboard.

After two or three failed attempts, the trans-Atlantic cable was successfully laid, but on September 5, 1858, after only one month of operation, communications failed, as did Mr. Field's portfolio. He did not waver, however, and by 1865 he had once again raised enough capital to set out to complete this nearly impossible endeavour, only to watch the new line break after 1,300 miles of cable had been laid.

Believe it or not, Field tried again and in 1866 he completed the task and the cable is still there today.

Mount Stephen viewed from the summit of Mount Field.

Emerald Lake in the distance from the west side slope
of Mount Field.

The tranquil village of Field, BC, is nestled along the
banks of the Kicking Horse River.

160

10. PAGET PEAK

An historic fire lookout, now used as a shelter for hikers, is perched on the side of the mountain. You can clearly see why this location was considered so strategic in the Parks department forest fire management policy. Breathtaking panoramas of the Kicking Horse Valley and the peaks of the Lake O'Hara region are understandable motives for choosing this location over two others. Most hikers stop at the comfort of the lookout, enjoy the view and go no farther, but surprisingly the scenery is even better at the top.

DIFFICULTY ▲ ▲
ELEVATION GAIN: 985 M

Trailhead:	GPS: N51 26 25.2 W116 21 17.7
	Elevation: 1601 m
Paget Lookout	GPS: N51 26 57.4 W116 22 05.8
	Elevation: 2104 m
Paget Peak Summit:	GPS: N51 27 34.6 W116 21 54.9
	Elevation: 2586 m

Trailhead: From the pretty little town of Field, drive 11 km east toward Lake Louise to the Wapta Lake picnic area, on the north (left) side of the highway. The signed trailhead is easy to find. If you have a half-hour to spare after your hike, venture into Field and explore the history, meet the locals and enjoy the ice cream.

From the parking lot, head into the forest, and within a few minutes (80 m) you will come to the first marked fork. Turn left and continue up the path in this beautiful subalpine forest for another 1.4 km, then turn left again at the last junction. Another 2.5-km ascent takes you to Paget Lookout. As usual with a hike below treeline, this one consists of switchbacks amid a magnificent forest. Although the trees obscure the view of neighbouring mountains, waterfalls and glaciers, the scenery within the

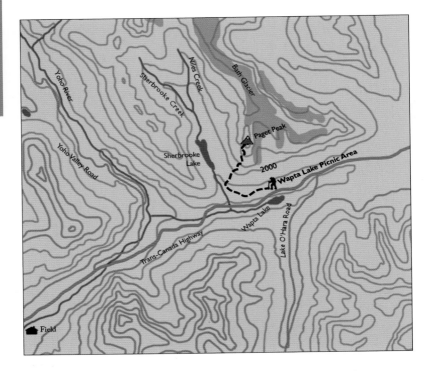

forest is just as rewarding. While walking, focus your senses, listening to the unique sounds and smells that are offered and the display of plant life on the forest floor. Soon you will notice the subtle change in vegetation as the forest thins out to shorter, leaner pine trees. Shortly afterward, you will be more than halfway to the summit, arriving at Paget Lookout.

Although the path narrows as it departs Paget Lookout, it is still well used and uncomplicated. But as it departs this remarkable structure, the trail becomes loose stone atop rough limestone. This pebbled surface is short-lived, but pockets of it reappear throughout the uphill trek. Always be careful on pebbles, of course, and be even more careful on the descent than on the ascent.

As the route gains more elevation, the first mistaken summit is seen directly upward, seemingly within easy reach. Do not be fooled into thinking the summit is as close as this. Once you achieve this rise, there is yet another one to overcome before you reach the actual summit. The trail becomes less trampled, presenting more rubble and shale the higher you climb.

Nearing the top of this exposed, moderately steep slope provides clear views of southern peaks and rivers and most notably the turquoise waters of Sherbrooke Lake to the west. Once at the summit, I'm sure you'll agree the rewards of this day's climb far outweigh the effort put in. To the southeast is Mount Victoria, with Mount Lefroy behind it. Just below and to the south are Wapta Lake and the Kicking Horse River.

Paget Peak history

Paget Peak is the only scramble in this guide that features an historic building. Dean Paget, a founding member of the Alpine Club of Canada, recorded the first ascent of this mountain with a group of climbers from the ACC. The fire lookout that bears his name was constructed more than half a century after his summit climb, as a result of two unforgiving fire seasons in the late 1930s and early 1940s. The lookout was in steady use until the late 1970s.

Sherbrooke Lake viewed from the slope of Paget Peak. I am certain it has the most-turquoise water I have ever seen.

11. MOUNT BURGESS

This gorgeous, scenic endeavour features views of the village of Field, Emerald Lake and Emerald Lake Lodge as well as of surrounding magnificent peaks. This peak is an easy, straightforward forest scramble until you come to an intimidating scree chute. The north summit is easily achieved, while the somewhat higher south peak is much more challenging. This route describes the north (lower) peak.

DIFFICULTY ▲ ▲ ▲
ELEVATION GAIN: 1320 M

Trailhead:	GPS: N51 24 17.3 W116 28 58.7
	Elevation: 1254 m
Mount Burgess Summit:	GPS: N51 25 35.0 W116 30 11.6
	Elevation: 2574 m

Trailhead: From the Yoho National Park Information Centre in Field, head east on the Trans-Canada Highway for 1.4 km. Turn left (north) onto the only unpaved road and immediately make a left at the first fork. Keep left for 400 m and the Burgess Pass trailhead will greet you.

Within the first couple of minutes you'll pass a rare find of natural springs, on your right. There seem to be two or three of these underground aquifers spouting from the hillside and beneath rotting logs. A fork in the path lies just beyond them. Choose the right-hand trail.

In a forest of Engelmann spruce and lodgepole pine, there are the occasional western red cedars that seem completely out of place. These sporadic trees are taller and thicker than the other evergreens and have distinctive grey, vertically lined bark.

About 500 m into the hike there is a short boardwalk of stairs consisting of about six long platforms. Although the boards are old, there is a distinct smell of damp, exposed wood when they are wet. This smell, combined with that of a few nearby western red cedars and a mossy forest floor, results in a unique scent unlike any other I have experienced in the Rockies.

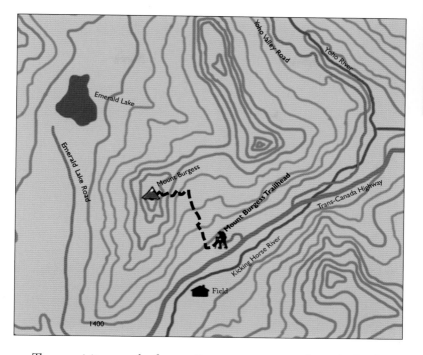

The exquisite sound of a small stream resonates through the forest as the hike begins a mild uphill climb, and within 20 minutes from the trailhead this stream exposes itself on your right. The path then leaves the stream as it begins a much steeper ascent, with sharp switchbacks interspersed with long flat stretches. You'll cross this same stream again in another 20 minutes or so, and it is the last source of water for the entire climb. Stop here and top up your thirst and canisters.

As the trail winds upward beyond the stream, the forest opens and the view of Field and its rocky guardians becomes ever clearer. This scenery makes the continual climbing tolerable. Another kilometre brings the path to a wide, dry avalanche trench. The power of tumbling snow is evident, as the underbrush and trees have been replaced by a broad swath of rock and rubble. To cross this debris field, follow cairns and a faint track. Once on the other side, follow the cairns up the avalanche slope until the trail into the forest reappears on your right. Someone from

165

Parks Canada has packed a chain saw up here to cut a convenient notch in a large fallen tree for us.

For another 45 minutes, the forest gradually thins and the trees become shorter as you reach the subalpine. Look for a tree on the right that has two distinct axe or hatchet wedges hacked from it. An additional 15 to 20 minutes past this tree, on the left side of the open hillside, is a faint track leading to the summit. There are piles of rocks on either side (GPS N51 24 56.0 W116 29 30.4; elevation 1783 m). From this spot, the faint track to the summit of Mount Burgess takes off to the left onto the exposed slope, toward an easily spotted island of trees.

As the trail winds upward on solid ground toward the tree island, keep to the right side of it. The ground is firmer there, with less talus. Beyond the island, the path becomes a long chute that has loose rubble in the middle, so again keep to the right whenever possible. There are a few minor rock bands that require climbing, but they are only a couple of metres high at best. The clambering through the chute becomes incessant and you'll emerge from it twice before the summit finally comes into view.

Across the Kicking Horse River, Mount Stephen looms so large that you feel you can reach across the valley and touch it. Emerald Lake sits below Mount Burgess to the northwest, while Mount Field is just next door to Mount Burgess, at $80°$ east.

Mount Burgess history

Alexander MacKinnon Burgess was Deputy Minister of the Interior in 1886 when Otto Klotz named Burgess Mountain and Burgess Pass for his superior officer. By 1897 Burgess had become the federal commissioner for public lands. The Burgess Shale fossil beds, discovered later in Burgess Pass, were also named after him.

Geologists and paleontologists have called the Burgess Shale the most significant fossil discovery in 100 years. The fossils' age – some 505 million years – and finely detailed preservation are unique in the world. The broad diversity of organisms, mainly trilobites and small, shrimplike creatures, flourished on a warm, shallow seabed. Mudslides periodically reburied the creatures, and over millions of years their remains turned to stone from the immense pressure of the overlying sediment that at one time was more than 10 km thick. As the Rocky Mountains were pushed upward about 175 million years ago, the ancient seabed also shot upward, putting the trilobites now atop a mountain pass.

The Burgess Shale was discovered by the secretary of the Smithsonian Institution, Charles Doolittle Walcott, on August 30, 1909. He had studied a much lesser bed on Mount Stephen in 1907, which had been found by Otto Klotz in 1886 on a horse trail in Burgess Pass.

J.J. McArthur was the first person to climb to the summit of Mount Burgess, in 1892. While surveying the Rocky and Selkirk ranges for the CPR, McArthur climbed many of the mountains throughout this vast region, claiming many first ascents as well. Mount McArthur in the Little Yoho Valley was named after him in 1886 by Otto Klotz.

In the midst of Yoho National Park the village of Field offers all amenities to restock your backpacking and scrambling supplies. They also have fantastic ice cream!

Mount Stephen seems very close from a forest
opening on the Mount Field trail.

The first several kilometres of the trail to the summits
of mounts Burgess and Field is an upward walk
through a fantastic forest of spruce and pine.

168

12. MOUNT NILES

This is an absolutely gorgeous walk in the wilderness, highlighted by a finale of a 600-m climb up a scree slope to easily reach the summit of Mount Niles. However, the long approach of approximately 10 km to the summit is just as satisfying as reaching the top of this magnificent peak. The visual, auditory and olfactory feast of meadows, waterfalls, lakes, streams, forest and flowers is stunning.

DIFFICULTY ▲ ▲ ▲ ▲
ELEVATION GAIN: 1369 M

Trailhead:	GPS: N51 26 25.2 W116 21 17.7
	Elevation: 1601 m
Mount Niles Summit:	GPS: N51 30 18.0 W116 25 18.1
	Elevation: 2970 m

Trailhead: The trailhead is on the north side of the Trans-Canada Highway, 11 km east of the town of Field, BC. Park in the Wapta Lake picnic area and you will easily locate the signs directing you to Sherbrooke Lake.

The first landmark is Sherbrooke Lake's blue and turquoise-green waters. The easy walk to the lake is only 3 km, with a mild uphill gain. Only a few minutes along, you'll come to the first fork and sign. Take the path to the left, as going right will take you back to the highway at West Louise Lodge. The elevation gain begins about 1 km from this intersection and continues for only about 500 m, placing you at another junction with good signage. Take the left fork to Sherbrooke Lake, with only 1.6 km left to go.

Less than a kilometre before the lake, a small clearing appears, affording you a fantastic view of Mount Ogden bordering the western shore of Sherbrooke Lake. Just beyond the clearing is an extended span of boardwalks raised slightly above the muddy earth. The trail provides a few points of access to the lake as it parallels the eastern shore, and within half an hour you will be at the far end of the lake, climbing up a small section of switchbacks.

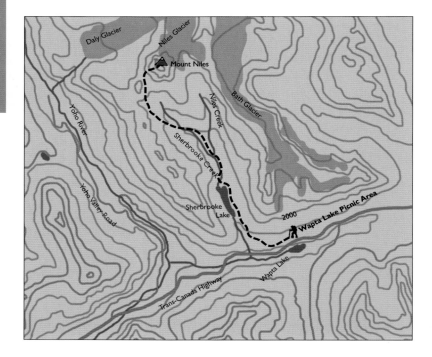

The path sticks to Sherbrooke Creek for the next 500 m as it meets a 20- to 25-m stepped waterfall. Our group was unaware of the existence of this cascade, so we were ecstatic with our discovery. We stopped and played here for 20 or 30 minutes before continuing our journey. This would turn out to be only the first of many spectacular waterfalls along the way, some almost within arm's reach, many others visible off in the distance. Another pleasant surprise came a few minutes later in the form of a long meadow on the banks of Sherbrooke Creek. It takes about 15 to 20 minutes to cross the expanse of this meadow filled with red paint brush and a variety of low-growth shrubs.

The path leaves the openness of the meadow for a forest and switchbacks that deliver more waterfalls along the way before meeting an exposed subalpine region of stunted trees and pastures another half-hour upward. There is some minor rockhopping and log walking required to cross the few streams that drain this area. Sticking to the trail for a further kilometre brings you to another small creek crossing at the base of a small, open, grassy meadow with the magnificent Mount Niles straight ahead. Directly across the valley, look for a rather large cairn that marks the start of an uphill battle. The cairn sits at the base of a drainage outlet that is usually dry. Walk up the drainage for about 50 m until you reach a well-defined track on the right. This path is a saviour of lungs, as it switchbacks up the hillside. If you miss this trail, there is no other way but straight up the dry gulch. An hour of hiking brings you to a rolling meadow that eventually hooks up with a scree slope at the base of the summit push. You have hiked 8.8 km from the trailhead.

The way from here is a straightforward jaunt across the base of the scree slope to the far left (west) side of Niles Knoll. The trail has faded, so make your own way across and up, wrapping around the far side. Upon successfully reaching the obvious col, continue on a path that progresses up to the top of the knoll along the summit ridge.

Views from this vantage point are overwhelming as the Wapta Icefield comes into view to the north and Mount Daly to the northeast, while directly south lies the wonderful valley you've just hiked up.

Mount Niles history

The mountain was named after William Harmon Niles by Charles S. Thompson in 1898. Niles was one of the first explorers to climb the mountains of the Yoho area. He was a professor of geology at Massachusetts Institute of Technology and served as president of the Appalachian Mountain Club. The first ascent of this wondrous peak was by D. Campbell and C.E. Fay in 1898.

Sherbrooke Lake on the journey to Mount Niles.

Streams and waterfalls are plentiful throughout Yoho
National Park. This spectacular cascade is viewed from
the Mount Niles trail.

13. MOUNT KERR

Very few scramblers attempt the true summit of Mount Kerr, because it requires so much more effort for only a handful of metres in elevation. The steep descent from the first summit and subsequent climb to the true summit requires some 4×4 scrambling combined with a bit of jumping from short ledges. The direct distance to the summit is quite significant as well, taking considerable time. The first summit is a remarkable peak that offers astonishing views of glaciated cirques. The decision is yours: once you arrive at the first summit, assess the worth of continuing beyond.

This ranks as one of the best-ever summit climbs, simply because the journey to the peak is astounding. The hour-long walk from Little Yoho Campground to Kiwetinok Pass is littered with meadows, streams, glaciers, waterfalls, moraines, mountains, a magnificent lake and a smattering of trees. Enjoy this magnificent walk. There are many like it, but none quite like it.

The trailhead elevation and elevation gain given here are calculated as from the Stanley Mitchell Hut.

DIFFICULTY ▲ ▲ ▲
ELEVATION GAIN: 745 M

Trailhead:	GPS: N51 31 36.0 W116 33 48.0
	Elevation: 2060 m
Mount Kerr Summit:	GPS: N51 30 32.7 W116 35 56.8
	Elevation: 2805 m

Trailhead: For directions to the Stanley Mitchell Hut, refer to the Little Yoho Campground hike.

With the Stanley Mitchell Hut as the starting point, get on the route toward the Iceline Trail and cross the Little Yoho River. Within five minutes from the river crossing, a sign to Kiwetinok Pass guides you to a gentle stroll along the river. This is short-lived, however, as a climb up a hillside interrupts this riverside walk. This ascent is just as short, but it

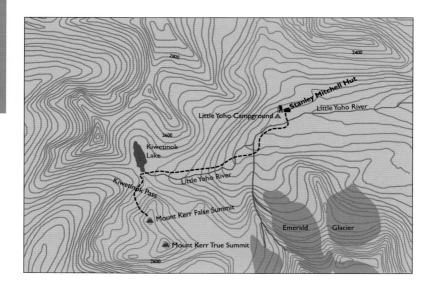

becomes well worth the five minutes of panting as the sky soon opens up out of the forest to reveal an incredible torrential river draining a glacier that is parked in a cirque up to your left.

This unnamed river – and the next one, the Little Yoho – must be crossed to achieve the summit of Mount Kerr. But there is a distinct lack of bridges to help you, so you are most likely going to get wet. Many hikers have placed logs and rocks here for easier crossing, but these contributions are still inadequate. Also, there are numerous trails leading uphill on the near side of both these rivers, especially the second one, but do not follow them. Make no mistake: you must cross both rivers, and these two major crossings are about five minutes apart.

We once ran into some fellow hikers here who apparently made this very mistake. They told us they were on their way back down from Kiwetinok Pass. But as we talked with them, we realized they could not have reached the pass. They were directing us to take the trail on the near side of the second river and follow it up to the pass, but when I asked about Kiwetinok Lake, they replied there was no lake. It was obvious they'd made a navigational error and could not possibly have reached the pass by the route they were recommending. They seemed happy with their day's accomplishment, though, so we saw no reason to set them straight. But the point here is that even though there is a well-trodden path up the near bank of the second river at this spot, you still have to cross the river.

On the far side of the second crossing, search out the abundance of cairns and follow them back downstream to pick up the main trail again. The path resumes in sparse forest and continues to climb gradually, with sporadic steep grades, up to an immense, treeless alpine that will stun you. Up here, the grade levels out substantially and is barely noticeable as you wander toward Kiwetinok Lake. Take time to look around and venture off track. A nifty little stream that empties the lake and surrounding glaciers cuts into the ground over to the south (your left), only 20 to 30 m away. Numerous small waterfalls populate the cool, tranquil stream that has cut its way through the solid limestone beneath the soil you are standing on. At some point, step across the small drainage stream of the lake. At Kiwetinok Lake you are visiting the highest named lake in Canada. To the left (west) of the lake is a quick 33-metre jaunt up to the summit of Kiwetinok Pass.

Head south (left) toward the north slope of Mount Kerr and look for a suitable route. Only 313 m of elevation remains before you conquer the first summit of Mount Kerr, and the way is strewn with cairns and trails. Since the slope is reasonably firm and lacks substantial scree, it is just a matter of following one of many paths to the summit. The only noteworthy formation is a modest col just before the summit.

You will not believe your own eyes. This is unquestionably some of the best scenery on the entire planet. Glaciers resting between peaks and clinging to the sides of mountains, glacier-worn rock, glacier-fed streams and many mountain peaks indulge the eyes. The President Range dominates the eastern sky and the Kiwetinok Range covers the western horizon. To the southeast, Mount Marpole appears to be within throwing distance 2.3 km away, with Mount Carnarvon twice that far almost due south. Your next goal, Mount Pollinger, lies directly north on the other side of Kiwetinok Lake.

Mount Kerr history

This mountain was first ascended by Edward Whymper in 1901, and in 1907 Whymper named the peak for Robert Kerr, a CPR passenger traffic manager who had helped publicize Whymper's arrival from England and his tourism-building travels throughout the Rockies and the Selkirks.

One of Kerr's responsibilities was to promote the railway's mountain destinations by bringing in big-name mountaineers and guides, and his greatest achievement was the importing of Edward Whymper, the celebrated British mountaineer credited with the first ascent of the Matterhorn. Kerr arranged to have all of Whymper's expenses covered by the CPR while in Canada promoting the railway and its hotels. For this effort, Whymper named Mount Kerr as a sign of his gratitude to his sponsor.

Two of Whymper's guides, Joseph Pollinger and Christian Kaufmann, expressed their desire to have the peak named after them. Whymper was steadfast, however, in naming not only this mountain for Kerr, but a second peak after another sponsor from the CPR, Richard Marpole. Whymper sealed the honour by inscribing the names on his official map.

In 1910, another Canadian place also became a namesake of Robert Kerr: the town of Kerrobert, Saskatchewan. Kerr's job as passenger traffic manager included the railway's Saskatchewan segment, and the town became a divisional point and trading centre for a large surrounding district at the time. The promise of further economic development fell short, however, and the community never really blossomed as expected. Today its population is about 1,000.

This interesting little stream eventually becomes
the Little Yoho River.

Kiwetinok Lake is the highest named lake in Canada.

177

14. MOUNT POLLINGER

Like the Mount Kerr scramble, the Mount Pollinger approach is enveloped in an abundance of mountain scenery. Everything you could hope to see is found along this trail. A gorgeous lake, glaciers, waterfalls, streams, moraines, meadows and forest are all on display, even before you reach the base of the mountain.

The trailhead elevation and elevation gain are calculated as from the Stanley Mitchell Hut.

DIFFICULTY ▲ ▲ ▲
ELEVATION GAIN: 761 M

Trailhead:	GPS: N51 31 36.0 W116 33 48.0
	Elevation: 2060 m
Mount Pollinger Summit:	GPS: N51 31 47.5 W116 35 55.8
	Elevation: 2821 m

Trailhead: For directions to the Stanley Mitchell Hut, please refer to the "Little Yoho Campground" hike.

Using the Stanley Mitchell Hut as your starting point, head south to find the route toward the Iceline Trail, and then cross the Little Yoho River on a solidly built post and beam bridge. Soon after crossing the river you will come across a sign directing you to Kiwetinok Pass. Following the trail indicated places you on a gentle riverside stroll, but only for a brief time. Enjoy the flat grade while you can, because before too long you'll begin to climb a fairly steep hillside. This section too is short-lived, but your upward exertion is thoroughly rewarded as you reach the next plateau and the forest breaks open to reveal an absolutely incredible sky. Up to the left, a cirque cradles a magnificent glacier whose melt water tumbles relentlessly over the rocks below. This, combined with a panorama blocked by a line of peaks and moraines, should cause your heart to skip a beat.

The melt water from the glacier field above gathers to form an unnamed river that tumbles across this exposed plateau. This river, and the next one,

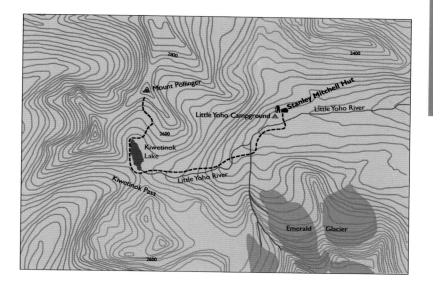

the Little Yoho River, must be crossed to achieve the summit of Mount Kerr. But there is a distinct lack of bridges to help you, so you are most likely going to get wet. Many hikers have placed logs and rocks here for easier crossing, but these contributions are still inadequate. Also, there are numerous trails leading uphill on the near side of both these rivers, especially the second one, but do not follow them. Make no mistake: you must cross both rivers, and these two major crossings are about five minutes apart.

We once ran into some fellow hikers here who apparently made this very mistake. They told us they were on their way back down from Kiwetinok Pass. But as we talked with them, we realized they could not have reached the pass. They were directing us to take the trail on the near side of the second river and follow it up to the pass, but when I asked about Kiwetinok Lake, they replied there was no lake. It was obvious they'd made a navigational error and could not possibly have reached the pass by the route they were recommending. They seemed happy with their day's accomplishment, though, so we saw no reason to set them straight. But the point here is that even though there is a well-trodden path up the near bank of the second river at this spot, you still have to cross the river.

On the far side of the second crossing, search out the abundance of cairns and follow them back downstream to pick up the main trail again. The path resumes in sparse forest and continues to climb gradually, with sporadic steep grades, up to an immense, treeless alpine that will stun you. Up here, the grade levels out substantially and is barely noticeable as you wander toward Kiwetinok Lake. Take time to look around and venture off track. Over to the south (your left), is a nifty little stream that empties the lake and surrounding glaciers and contributes to the birth of the Little Yoho River. Numerous small waterfalls festoon this cool, tranquil stream that has cut its way through the solid limestone beneath the soil you are standing on. It will be necessary to step across this small drainage stream at some point as you approach Kiwetinok Lake, the highest named lake in Canada.

Take a look northward at the slope at the far end of the lake to establish the route you will take up this hillside. Kiwetinok Peak is the striking pinnacle to the left (west) and Mount Pollinger is the summit seen to the right. Between the two, there appears to be a selection of ascents, but the easiest and safest route is the least conspicuous one. The three chutes that are in plain sight are *not* the way to go. They are too steep and provide limited footing. The clear slope to the far left of the chutes, past the rock bands, should be avoided as well. It looks unencumbered at first, but it leads straight to the dead end of the uppermost wall.

The correct course lies to the right of the right-hand chute. There is a series of horizontal limestone belts that must be overcome. Bypass these around their eastern (right) side. Now backtrack, heading west, without climbing (laterally), to reach a small gap in the uppermost belt. Once through this gap, there is a brief hike to the ridge between the two peaks.

To get there and begin the climb, make your way to the far end of the lake by walking the left shoreline. The descent can be quite dangerous if you decide not to come down this same route. The rock belts are high in spots, and loose rock with narrow ledges should be avoided. I suggest you visually and mentally mark the gap on your way up, so you can find it again on your way back down.

From the ridge the remaining distance to the summit is 320 m to the east, with only 44 m of elevation left to climb. From the summit, Mount Amiskwi is 6.6 km due west, and Mount McArthur is a stone's throw away to the north.

Preferred route up Mount Pollinger.

Mount Pollinger history

Edward Whymper and Joseph Pollinger came to the Canadian Rockies together from England in 1901. Officially Pollinger became one of Whymper's four guides throughout his various climbs in the Rockies, but there were some differing opinions in camp as to what was expected of one another.

Pollinger and the three other guides, Christian Klucker, Christian Kaufmann (Kaufmann Lake) and Joseph Bossonney, were adamant that they were professional mountaineer guides, not cooks or porters. This created some friction during the expeditions, but regardless the party still managed to make first ascents of Mount Whymper, Mount Kerr and Stanley Peak. While in their Vermilion camp on June 29, 1901, Whymper wrote in his journal, as quoted in Roger Patillo's *The Canadian Rockies*:

Instructed my people to camp at once as I feared rain and snow but Pollinger and Kaufmann sulked and did nothing and said they wanted food. They did nothing, however, toward preparing it, and when it was ready I observed how hungry they were by going off fishing, without partaking of it.

Prior to coming to Canada, Whymper's biggest accomplishment was being the first to ascend the Matterhorn. After eight failed attempts, he summited on July 14, 1865.

Looking north from Mount Kerr: Kiwetinok Peak on the left, Kiwetinok Lake and Mount Pollinger on the right.

This stunning view is to enjoy en route to Kiwetinok Pass.

15. NARAO PEAK

This scramble is broken up into three distinct sections. The first is an uphill trudge with bushwhacking through an unmarked forest. The middle part is an uphill trudge on an alpine hillside, while the third section is an uphill trudge of loose scree skirting around rock walls. Quite a lot of uphill trudging there. The scramble also features some distinct exposure and there are some decisions to be made about how to get around two of the largest obstacles. These can be avoided by dropping down to the right of them, or you can try your scrambling skills up and over them. There are three summits: one minor, one false and one true, and all of them lie along a superb ridge walk. Sound like fun? This is an immense day, so leave early and make sure to take some energy supplement. This will be a day of serious exertion.

DIFFICULTY ▲ ▲ ▲ ▲
ELEVATION GAIN: 1245 M FROM ROSS LAKE TRAILHEAD

Trailhead:	GPS: N51 26 41.4 W116 19 44.5
	Elevation: 1608 m
Ross Lake Trailhead:	GPS: N51 25 50.4 W116 20 37.4
	Elevation: 1730 m
Narao Peak Summit:	GPS: N51 24 39.0 W116 18 52.8
	Elevation: 2975 m

Trailhead: Take the Trans-Canada Highway 13.5 km east of Field and follow the highway markers to the Lake O'Hara parking lot. Hike 2 km up the Lake O'Hara road (distances are marked on trees on the right-hand side). There you'll see a couple of different entrances into the forest. The first one is five minutes down the Ross Lake Trail, which lies just before the 2-km marker. The second entrance is just past the marker, where the woods open ever so slightly.

The first leg of this scramble has neither a real trail nor a marked trailhead, so bushwhacking is your only option for reaching the summit.

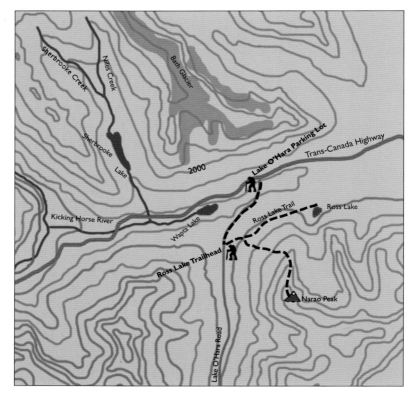

Walking up the road presents terrific views of the approach to Narao Peak. It also provides a plan of attack on the forest: once you are in the woods, the summit is not visible, so try to gain a general sense of where you are going before entering blindly. Still, it is difficult to get turned around, since the only two directions are either up or down. Nonetheless, it is possible to emerge from the woods too far north of the scree slope, which would entail some doubling back. There is close to two hours of pushing through the forest on a severe uphill grade, and there is plenty of low-level vegetation that has the sole purpose of cutting up your shins, so be careful. Dress accordingly.

The climb up to treeline presents you with a massive slope of alpine growth of lichens and flowers, fist-size rocks and solid soil for firm footing.

This is a long, exhausting push on this slope, and you will already be quite weary from hacking your way through the bush. The idea is to attain the ridge as soon as possible, as walking the ridge is comparatively easier.

The ridge walk has an easy grade and even some flat spots, which is comparatively substantial relief, considering how you've just spent your morning. This sauntering style of ridge walking is soon disturbed by various rock buttresses, with two of them presenting clear problems. Having said that, they can all be quite easily evaded by detouring around the right side of them. If you do choose the detours, however, you will have to clamber back up to regain the ridge, involving considerably more work. There is one intimidating rock band in particular (the first substantial one you meet) that can be bypassed like the others, but this one should be ascended by a conveniently placed chimney chute at the right side of the buttress. Upon exiting the chimney, regain the ridge by moving carefully to the left on a ledge.

Ultimately, scrambling over and around the variety of hurdles will place you at all three summits, including the false (north) and the true (south) summits. Gaining the true summit will require you to drop down from the false summit into a col and then up a moderate slope of large rocks and scree.

This is a day that will be a standout for you for a long, long time. Probably because of the amount of work it took, or maybe the views, this

Preferred route up Narao Peak.

day will become a shining moment in your life. You should be proud of yourself.

The scenery is certainly worthy of the effort. Imagine seeing Mount Victoria, Mount Niles, Sherbrooke Lake, Cathedral Mountain, Mount Goodsir, Paget Peak, the Waputik Icefield and Mount Bosworth all by simply turning your head. What a day!

This spectacular panorama from the western slope of Narao Peak includes, left to right, Vanguard Peak, Narao Lakes and Wapta Lake.

Ross Lake. Yoho National Park.

Narao Peak history

Narao Peak was named by the Interprovincial Boundary Survey in 1916. Narao, a Stoney Indian word, has been loosely translated to mean "hit in the stomach." This more than likely refers to the incident of James Hector being kicked by a horse while travelling up the Kicking Horse River in 1858. The Interprovincial Boundary Commission first ascended this peak while surveying these local mountains in 1913.

Unnamed knoll on the eastern shore of Ross Lake.

Narao Peak's scree slope. This is only one segment of a hard day to the summit.

16. MOUNT WHYMPER

This is a moderately difficult scramble with significant challenges, as there are several stout rock walls that will call upon minor scrambling skills, making this a complete pleasure to climb. Many logbooks and various sources state that the least problematic way around the rockbands is to find a route that suits you. Take the time to explore the face of the daunting main wall near the summit, and do not be afraid to backtrack if your first choice becomes too difficult.

DIFFICULTY ▲ ▲ ▲ ▲ ▲
ELEVATION GAIN: 1262 M

Trailhead:	GPS: N51 12 19.7 W116 04 50.6
	Elevation: 1581 m
Mount Whymper Summit:	GPS: N51 13 27.1 W116 05 52.9
	Elevation: 2843 m

Trailhead: The trailhead parking lot is easily reached on the south side of the Banff–Windermere Highway (Hwy. 93), 13 km from Castle Junction. It is marked as the Stanley Glacier Trail parking lot, and like so many scrambles in the mountain parks, there is no reference to Mount Whymper at all. I will direct you there.

Mount Whymper is easily spotted from the highway, as it lies slightly back from the northwest side of it. Walk back up the highway toward Castle Junction, 500 m from the parking lot, until you reach the opening of an avalanche slope. This opening is the culmination of debris from two gullies farther up that will eventually narrow to chutes as they approach the top of the mountain. The main channel is the one on the right, and you will need to make your way over to it before too long.

As destructive as avalanches can be, they have a tendency to leave re-markable scenery in their wake as they tear apart hillsides that were once populated by a forest. The wide open slope delivers amazing views of Storm Mountain and Stanley Peak across the highway. Within 90 minutes

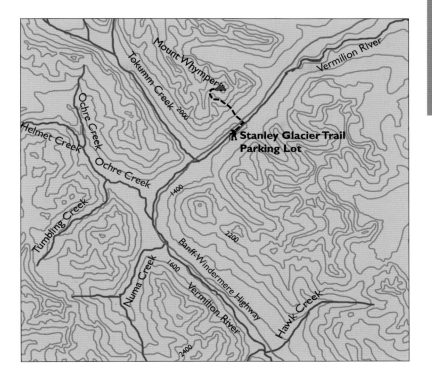

of toiling up the gulley, you come to the first of a few easy scrambles over minor rock bands. It is best to veer to the right side of the first of these. The remaining obstacles are barely worth mentioning.

More clambering upward on loose rubble brings you to a high, narrow limestone buttress that splits the gulley, creating two distinctive routes. The left path is the recommended one. Make your way through the chute around the left side of the rock edifice and emerge through the gully, keeping to the left for the easiest course over more rock bands. Route-finding now becomes somewhat tricky, and you will soon discover that there are many ways to go. However, after veering to the left, it seems that the least troublesome approach is directly up the middle of the rockband. Regardless, you will be confronted with some hand over fist exposure.

I usually feel compelled to inform readers when they will encounter a tough or even dangerous part of a scramble and this is one of those moments. I do not enjoy spending the day on a slippery scree slope only to discover that the final 30 m are beyond my sense of well-being. There is significant exposure at this point of the journey, so assess your comfort level. Even stop to envision the descent. You are almost at the summit, but do not push yourself; it is only a mountain and there are plenty of other ones to conquer. From experience, I cannot stress how important it is to have a pact with yourself and your buddies prior to reaching a summit. In our crew, we have an ironclad verbal agreement that if one of us is not feeling comfortable about a section of a climb, then the day is over. There is no discussion and there is certainly no argument about it. Everyone understands.

Fortunately, no one objected on this day, so we scrambled over the rock wall and quickly reached the summit.

Mount Whymper history

Edward Whymper gained notoriety for his first ascent of the Matterhorn in 1865. The CPR brought him to the Rockies to do some climbing for publicity purposes, but his efforts fell far short of his earlier achievements. He and his entourage of guides – Joseph Pollinger (Mount Pollinger), Christian Klucker, Christian Kaufmann (Kaufmann Lake) and Joseph Bossonney, explored the Rocky, Selkirk and Vermilion areas and ascended several peaks there, including Mount Whymper.

Soon after this well-publicized exploration had taken place, outfitters like Walter Nixon began transporting tourists through these valleys on horseback, blazing many trails that are still used today.

Mount Whymper, seen from the Stanley Glacier Trail
parking lot.

When you're struggling up a scree slope, turn around
every so often to enjoy the sights behind you. Here's
Stanley Peak viewed from the scree slope of Mount
Whymper. This rock outcropping is easily accessed, and
provides a fantastic spot for resting and viewing.

191

17. VERMILION PEAK

Vermilion Peak is best described as a straightforward, relatively quick scramble that starts ascending almost immediately. There is no warm up here, just right down to business. The drawback with this type of climb is that there is no break in it; it is just straight upward with no levelling off until you reach the summit.

DIFFICULTY ▲ ▲ ▲ ▲
ELEVATION GAIN: 1207 M

| Trailhead: | GPS: N51 09 35.6 W116 09 09.0 |
| | Elevation: 1419 m |

| Vermilion Peak Summit: | GPS: N51 09 37.3 W116 07 00.5 |
| | Elevation: 2586 m |

Trailhead: From the Castle Mountain junction on the Trans-Canada Highway follow Hwy. 93 (Banff–Radium Highway) 21 km south to 4.1 km south of the Marble Canyon parking lot and 1.5 km south of the Paint Pots parking lot. The trailhead is unmarked but you can recognize it by an opening in the forest creating a bit of a meadow on the east (left) side of the highway. It's your choice whether to park your vehicle here and leave it alone or park instead in the Paint Pots parking lot and walk the 1.5 km to the trailhead.

Cross this sometimes muddy field and follow the small slope up to the remnants of the old highway. Turn south (right) here and walk for about 75 to 100 m, reaching a wide opening in the forest on your left. This obvious, broad gap makes its way up to the gully, which you will remain in for the better part of this scramble. In fact, this gully is visible from the highway and is clearly the only choice up this side of the mountain.

This avalanche channel has two easy obstacles to manoeuvre. Two small rock walls in quick succession require a little bit of handwork for about 15 to 20 m. Beyond the rock walls, continue up the path and you will eventually encounter a fork. Both trails will bring you to the same

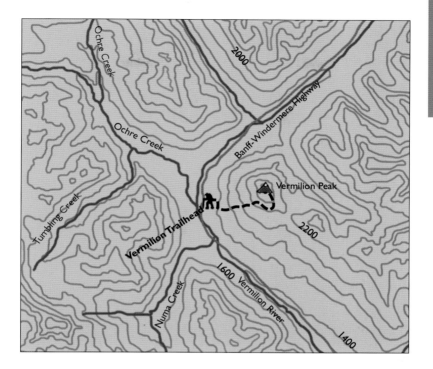

place. The right-hand one is shorter but steeper. Regardless which one you choose, you will arrive below the summit ridge. Continue ascending but begin to traverse to the right until you reach a reasonable approach that will get you to the summit ridge.

Once up on the ridge, most of the work is done and the rest is an easy walk on a well-trodden path that straddles the ridge to the summit. About 100 m shy of the cairn-marked true summit is the well-marked "popular" summit where most scramblers seem to stop due to exposure and sudden drops down either side. It is up to you. Assess your confidence and comfort and do not just go on pride.

Stanley Peak is unmistakable to the east at an impressive 3155 m, while the less impressive Mount Haffner is slightly south (right) at 2514 m.

Vermilion Peak history

Vermilion Peak derives its name from the river and valley of the same name. Vermilion is one of the brilliant colours of the pigment the Ktunaxa (Kootenay) First Nations discovered in this area. The Ktunaxa would extract the stuff from the region's ochre beds and heat it over large fires to smelt out the pigmented powder. They would then mix this with animal grease and use it for colouring their clothing, painting their bodies and making pictures on rocks. The most common colours were red (vermilion) and yellow.

Vermilion Peak. Kootenay National Park. The route to the summit is apparent from the roadside.

18. STORM MOUNTAIN

This is without doubt the toughest climb in this guide. This is the challenge that will graduate you from an aspiring scrambler to an accomplished one. There are countless kilometres of deadfall to climb over, bushwhacking to endure, route-finding to navigate, a boulder field to crawl over and a stream to splash across. But the best prize of this challenge is 1000 m of the nastiest scree you have ever encountered. This could possibly be the most exhausting day of your life.

DIFFICULTY ▲ ▲ ▲ ▲ ▲
ELEVATION GAIN: 1521 M

Trailhead: GPS: N51 13 06.1 W116 03 25.7
                       Elevation: 1644 m

Storm Mountain Summit: GPS: N51 12 27.6 W116 00 17.9
                        Elevation: 3165 m

Trailhead: From the crossroads of the Trans-Canada and the Banff–Windermere highways (Hwys. 1 and 93), travel south for 11.4 km to a small gravel pull-off on the east (left) side of the highway. This is readily recognized, as there is a steel gate inside the pull-off. This parking area is 1.2 km south of the Continental Divide marker, also on the east side of the parkway. The Continental Divide point of interest is 10.2 km south of Castle Junction.

Walk around the steel gate, follow the road and immediately enter a large field. Stroll through the middle of it and make your way to the far left end. Here there is a short, narrow gully taking you down to a stream that is barely too wide to step across. A makeshift bridge of old logs is apparent but slippery. Be careful. Waist-high brush presents the first obstacle for a trail-less beginning.

Past the thick brush, the way opens to the horrific remnants of the 2003 forest fire season and the repetitive deadfall that must be climbed over. This alone becomes exhausting after the first 40 or 50 of these natural

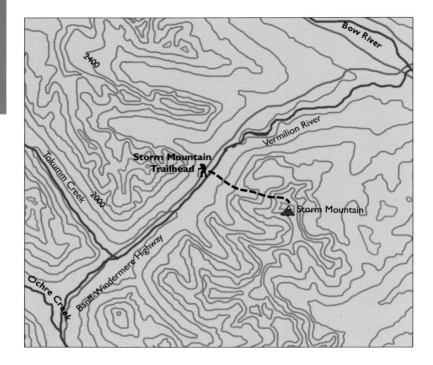

obstacles. The stream remains on your right as the trail ventures upward through burnt forest with green undergrowth. Stick close to the stream while searching for a faded track. It is there, so keep an eye out as you continue upward, because about 20 minutes into the trek you'll find a stack of cairns approximately knee high close to the stream. This marks the beginning of the recognizable trail.

From the cairns, the hike begins a five- to ten-minute ascent of switchbacks, eventually levelling off and leaving the stream below. After about five minutes of flat walking, the climbing resumes again. As the path weaves upward through the scorched forest, the obstacle course of fallen trees becomes quite tiresome. Over, under and around. Roughly another 20 minutes later, the forest begins to thin, the trees begin to shorten, and luckily the grade of the slope begins to decrease. Another ten minutes of bashing around deadfall and the trail and the stream meet once more.

Continue to follow the indistinct path for another 15 minutes as it tries its best to stay beside the stream, and you will be rewarded again by hurdling over still more fallen trees.

Now the forest opens to a magnificent, long boulder field situated right in the gully you've been hiking in as it approaches the base of the mountain. Looking upward to the right, the source of these large boulders becomes obvious. Different obstacles must now be negotiated as deadfall and brush give way to large rocks and massive boulders. The rockhopping begins about 90 minutes into this demanding journey. Initially contained inside the boulder gully, the path stays close to the forest on your left, but as the gully expands, the necessity of crossing this minefield of over-sized rocks becomes apparent. Watch for another gulch that enters yours, roughly 20 minutes into the boulder field. From this point, make your way to the right, over huge rocks the size of cars. It's quite fun, actually, once you establish a rhythm. Not so much fun when the lichen-encrusted rocks are wet and slippery, though, so be careful.

Believe it or not, accomplishing this boulder crossing has only put you in position to scramble up 900 to 1000 m of horrible, horrible, horrible scree. You have been warned, so please do not curse me out halfway up. In all of our discussions with fellow scramblers, when Storm Mountain comes up, it is immediately dismissed as the one that everyone is putting off. The rumours of this scree slope are legendary. And, yes, they are true.

The remainder of the hike is a trudge upward on a giant slope of rocks, pebbles, stones and gravel. "Upward" is obvious, but there is a best route to follow. As you enter the talus slope, you will see a path that has been traced by the drudgery of others. Continue up the belly of the slope, looking for a couple of prominent rock bands several hundred metres up. Stay to the right of these, eventually crossing over the top of them and moving to your left. As you cross leftward over the top of these rock bands, a cliff face is now on your right. Ultimately, you will bypass this by staying left and continue straight up again. As the false summit comes into view you'll easily see a large cairn slightly to the left. Direct yourself toward this cairn.

At some point you will need to ascertain your position on a mountainside of sliding rock that is simply working you into a state of fatigue.

Stop. Take many breaks. Look behind you and enjoy where you are. Gaze out and realize, as you look down at the highway, just how lucky you are. Watch the traffic whiz by, and become aware of your surroundings. You are one of less than one tenth of one tenth of one per cent of travellers that actually get out and do this. Then turn around and get back to work.

The route-finding really is not that difficult; just make sure you follow the trails on the scree to avoid heading into a dead canyon. From the cairn, the summit is still another 250 m up, but as the ascent continues, the grade decreases. Finally you begin to walk on reasonably level ground to approach the true summit over to your right.

Mount Ball's fantastic snow-covered peak, 6 km to the south, appears to hang over the summit of Storm Mountain, and with its apex at over 3300 m, it is incredibly impressive. To the west are Mount Whymper and Boom Mountain.

Storm Mountain history

Storm Mountain was first successfully climbed by W.S. Drewry and A. St. Cyr and their guide, Tom Wilson, in 1889. The peak was named by George M. Dawson in 1884. Many of Dawson's explorations to the region had him camped beneath the mountain, and bad weather seems to have been a theme during his visits here.

Dawson, a geologist, anthropologist, author, teacher, civil servant, geographer and paleontologist, was born in Nova Scotia and schooled at McGill College in Montreal, the Royal School of Mines in London and with the Geological Survey of Great Britain. Dawson was teaching chemistry at Morrin College in Quebec when, in 1872, he obtained a position with the Geological Survey of Canada, which brought him out West.

Dawson's two seasons of exploration, in 1883 and '84, yielded an incredibly accurate map of the Canadian Rockies from the Red Deer Valley and Kicking Horse Pass down to the US border. This meticulous map was published in 1886. One noteworthy prize collected during Dawson's time in the Kicking Horse area was the discovery of a Lower Cambrian trilobite, *Olenellus gilberti*, along the CPR main line, a quarter of a century before the discovery of the Burgess Shale.

Throughout his career, Dawson's surveying skills and mapmaking techniques became legendary. In fact, while in present-day Yukon in 1887 his talents foresaw extensive gold deposits. Ten years later, his maps and information were partially responsible for the Yukon gold rush.

George Dawson's achievements required significant physical endurance and agility. But he also had an exceptional mind and unwavering dedication, and he did more to advance the biological and geological study of western and northern Canada than any other single person in history. This would be an incredible undertaking for any individual, but more so for Dawson, as he lived with Pott's disease (tuberculosis of the spine), which gave him a deformed spine and a stunted body the size of a 12-year-old boy's.

It's a long day to the summit of Storm Mountain. Looking back, retracing the route, this view is from halfway up a 1000-m talus hill. A stream must be navigated, the forest from the highway requires bushwhacking over deadfall, and a boulder field must be crossed (you can see a dark patch of it below the cliffs on the left). Finally, there is the dreadful talus slope to deal with.

Acknowledgements

I have dedicated this book to my father, Pat Shea, who always encouraged me to follow my heart even if I did not know where it was taking me.

This series of books could not have been realized without the support of my wife, Debbie. She continuously strengthens and inspires my passion for hiking and scrambling. This project and the entire series requires time, travel, work, preparation, late nights, early mornings, research and dedication, and without her understanding, I would never have embraced such an incredible undertaking.

I could not have ventured far off the highways if I was not accompanied by my children, Tyler, Brock and Kelly Shea. I love you all so much. Thank you for joining me.

Nor could I have ventured far into the backcountry without my hiking companions Don Brown, Peter Peller and Nolan Brown. They are all lovers of the wilderness and are the best people to have with me. I am so happy that they all let me share their friendship.

Peter, Tyler, Don and Nolan have been equally gracious with their companionship to join me on many scrambles. Thanks for waiting for me when I fall behind, guys!

Brent Miller from Kamloops, BC, must be recognized for educating me many years ago. At the time, Brent owned and operated Outdoor Bound Clothing & Equipment, a sport outfitting store. He was patient with me and managed to enlighten and educate me so that I would never have an uncomfortable journey.

Derek Learmouth has donated an amazing amount of his own time to train me on how to use Adobe Photoshop and Illustrator properly. His professional guidance has allowed me to easily understand the education he has given me. He has selflessly sat with me at his computer for many hours demonstrating shortcuts, techniques and tips that I was not aware of. Thanks, Derek.

Having a tremendous friend like Peter Peller as a resource has also been an enormous asset. Peter is a librarian at the University of Calgary and has a degree in geology. His mapping skills have been a great contribution, his geology background has saved me hours of research, and his memory recall is exceptional. This book would not have materialized without him.

Many thanks also to Diane Thompson, library manager at Natural Resources Canada Library in Vancouver, for her tremendous assistance in helping me determine the age of Kinney Lake and the geological period when it was carved out of the earth by glaciation. Diane also enlisted the help of a staff geologist, for which I am also grateful. Their quick response and dedicated research combined to save me many, many hours of exhaustive research. Thank you!

The Journey

Dust arising from the path a new
journey to begin
From the peak to the base, the hills cast
a shadow upon us, as if to grin
Stating their difficulties, we look upon
in awe,
a quest, a trek, a challenge for all
The sweat and the pain; outweighed
by the lush fields, the sweet pure water,
and the rugged terrain
The icy guardians, they lurk up high in
the hills,
watching our every move, grumbling,
they stay still
Pushing through the rain, the snow and the sleet,
the body is tired.
Your eyes demand more
despite your sore feet
And when the sun comes up, your picture is
perfect, nothing you could have imagined,
and now the journey becomes worth it.

—Tyler Shea

Glossary

alluvial fan.	A fan-shaped accumulation of silt, sand, gravel and boulders deposited by fast-flowing mountain rivers when they reach flatter land.
alluvial plain.	A level or gently sloping tract or a slightly undulating land surface produced by extensive deposition of alluvium, usually adjacent to a river that periodically overflows its banks. May be situated on a flood plain, in a delta or in an alluvial fan.
alluvium.	A fine-grained fertile soil consisting of mud, silt and sand deposited by flowing water on flood plains, in riverbeds and in estuaries. Generally considered a young deposit in terms of geologic time.
alpine.	Living or growing on mountains above the treeline.
bear pole.	A pole or cable between two trees, used for hoisting food out of the reach of bears.
buttress.	A spur or projection on the side of a mountain.
cairn.	A pile of stones, usually conical in shape, raised as a landmark or memorial. In prehistoric times, cairns were usually erected over a grave. For scrambling and hiking, cairns are used for marking trails.
campground.	A designated area for camping, ideally consisting of outhouse(s), bear pole, common cooking/eating area, water source, designated grey-water area, and tent pads.
campsite.	A spot in a campground to set up a tent.
chimney.	A vertical fissure large enough for a person's body to enter.
chute.	An inclined trough, passage or channel through or down which objects may pass.
cirque.	A steep, bowl-shaped hollow at the upper end of a mountain valley, especially one forming the head of a glacier or stream.
col.	A depression in a ridge or range of mountains, generally affording a pass from one slope to another.
glacier.	A perennial mass of ice which moves over land. A glacier forms in locations where the mass accumulation of snow and ice exceeds ablation over many years.
grey-water area.	A common designated area at a campground where used water can be discarded.

icefield.	An area of ice less than 50,000 km^2 (19,305 mi.^{2}) in size often found in colder climates and at higher altitudes of the world where there is sufficient precipitation. It is an extensive area of interconnected valley glaciers from which the higher peaks rise as nunataks. Ice fields are larger than alpine glaciers, smaller than ice sheets and similar in area to icecaps.
limestone.	A sedimentary rock consisting mainly of calcium carbonate, deposited as the calcareous remains of marine animals or chemically precipitated from the sea.
moleskin.	A soft material, often with an adhesive backing, used especially on the feet to protect against chafing.
moraine.	A buildup of rocks and boulders deposited by a glacier.
nunatak.	An isolated mountain peak projecting through the surface of surrounding glacial ice and supporting a distinct fauna and flora after recession of the ice.
privy.	An outdoor toilet, usually consisting of a pole fastened between two trees for sitting on.
scree.	Loose debris consisting of rocks or sand covering the slope of a hill.
Spenco 2nd Skin™.	Moist-wound bandage.
subalpine.	Of, relating to, inhabiting or growing in mountainous regions just below treeline.
talus.	Rock fragments that have accumulated at the base of a cliff or slope. The concave slope formed by such an accumulation of rock fragments is called a talus slope.
tarn.	A small mountain lake formed by glaciers.
treeline.	The zone, at high altitudes or high latitudes, beyond which no trees grow.

See also, for example:

www.abc-of-mountaineering.com/mountaineering-dictionary.asp
www.santiamalpineclub.org/mountain/climbing/terms
www.thefreedictionary.com
http://dictionary.reference.com
www.answers.com

Bibliography

Akrigg, G.P.V., and Helen Akrigg. *1001 British Columbia Place Names*. Vancouver: Discovery Press, 1969.

Akrigg G.P.V., and Helen Akrigg. *British Columbia Place Names*. Vancouver: UBC Press, 1997.

Alpine Club of Canada. "Past Presidents." www.alpineclubofcanada.ca/whoweare/pastpresidents.html, accessed 20101020.

Berry, Oliver, and Brendan Sainsbury. *Banff, Jasper & Glacier National Parks*. London: Lonely Planet, 2008.

Brink, Nicky, and Stephen R. Bown. *Forgotten Highways: Wilderness Journeys Down the Historic Trails of the Canadian Rockies*. Victoria, BC: Brindle & Glass, 2007.

Bumsted, J.M. *Fur Trade Wars: The Founding of Western Canada*. Winnipeg: Great Plains Publications, 1999.

Burchinshaw, Dorothy. *Pioneers of Revelstoke*. Revelstoke, BC: Revelstoke Senior Citizens Assn., 1986.

Chalmers, J. W. *Fur Trade Governor: George Simpson, 1820-1860*. Edmonton: Institute of Applied Art, 1960.

Coleman, A.P. *The Canadian Rockies: New and Old Trails*. Mountain Classics Collection no. 1. Surrey, BC: Rocky Mountain Books, 2006.

Dempsey, Hugh A. *The CPR West: The Iron Road and the Making of a Nation*. Vancouver: Douglas & McIntyre, 1984.

Jenish, D'Arcy. *Epic Wanderer: David Thompson and the Mapping of the Canadian West*. Toronto: Doubleday Canada, 2004.

Jenkins, Phil, and George M. Dawson. *Beneath My Feet: The Memoirs of George Mercer Dawson*. Toronto: McClelland & Stewart, 2007.

Lahey, Dale. *George Simpson: Blaze of Glory*. Toronto: Dundurn Press, 2010.

Lakusta, Ernie. *The Intrepid Explorer: James Hector's Explorations in the Canadian Rockies*. Calgary: Fifth House, 2007.

Lothian, William F. *A Brief History of Canada's National Parks*. Ottawa: Supply & Services Canada, 1987.

Mackie, Richard Somerset. *Trading beyond the Mountains: The British Fur Trade on the Pacific, 1793–1843*. Vancouver: UBC Press, 1997.

Nobbs, Ruby M. *Revelstoke: History and Heritage*. Altona, Man.: Friesens, 1998.

Patillo, Roger W. *The Canadian Rockies: Pioneers, Legends and True Tales*. Victoria, BC: Trafford, 2005.

Patton, Brian: *Tales from the Canadian Rockies*. Toronto: McClelland & Stewart, 1993. First published Edmonton: Hurtig, 1984.

Putnam, William Lowell, Glen W. Boles, Roger W. Laurilla. *Place Names of the Canadian Alps*. Revelstoke, BC: Footprint, 1990.

———. *The Great Glacier and Its House: The Story of the First Center of Alpinism in North America, 1885–1925*. American Alpine Club, 1982.

Rayburn, Alan. *A Dictionary of Canadian Place Names*. 2nd ed. Don Mills, Ont.: Oxford University Press, 2010.

Rich, E.E. *The Fur Trade and The Northwest to 1857*. Toronto: McClelland & Stewart, 1967.

Simpson, George. *Part of Dispatch from George Simpson Esqr, Governor of Ruperts Land to the Governor & Committee of the Hudson's Bay Company London. March 1, 1829. Continued and Completed March 24 and June 5, 1829.* Edited by E.E. Rich, with an introduction by W. Stewart Wallace. Toronto: The Champlain Society, 1947.

Smith, James K. *Wilderness of Fortune: The Story of Western Canada.* Vancouver: Douglas & McIntyre, 1983.

Spry, Irene M. *The Palliser Expedition.* Calgary: Fifth House, 1995.

Stokes, Charles W. *Round About the Rockies: An Everyday Guide to the Rocky and Selkirk Mountains of Canada.* Toronto: Musson, 1923.

Woods, John G. *Glacier Country: Mount Revelstoke and Glacier National Parks.* Vancouver: Douglas & McIntyre, in co-operation with Environment Canada, Parks, 1987.

Yorath, Chris. *How Old Is That Mountain? A Visitor's Guide to the Geology of Banff and Yoho National Parks.* Madeira Park, BC: Harbour Publishing, 2006.

Index

More Titles from Rocky Mountain Books

The Aspiring Hiker's Guide 1
Mountain Treks in Alberta

Gerry Shea

This first volume in The Aspiring Hiker's Guide series is meant to encourage beginner and intermediate hikers, backpackers and scramblers to step into and explore the backcountry in Banff National Park, Lake Louise, Jasper National Park, Kananaskis Country and the Icefields Parkway with both confidence and excitement.

ISBN 978-1-897522-79-0
Colour Photos, Maps
$26.95, Softcover

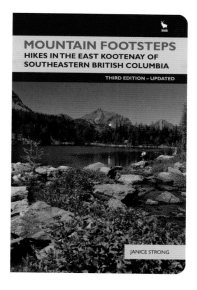

Mountain Footsteps

Hikes in the East Kootenay of Southeastern British Columbia
Third Edition – Updated

Janice Strong

Mountain Footsteps is one of Rocky Mountain Books' bestselling hiking guides. Covering routes around Cranbrook, Kimberley, Creston, Invermere, Radium and Fernie, located between the Rocky Mountains in the east and the Purcell Mountains in the west, including the Akamina Kishinena, Top of the World, Elk Lakes, St. Mary's Alpine and Bugaboo Glacier Provincial Parks, this volume will entice hikers of all abilities. As with previous editions, readers will continue to appreciate the author's detailed descriptions and personal anecdotes related to one of the most stunning areas in western Canada.

ISBN 978-1-926855-29-5

Colour Photos, Maps

$26.95, Softcover

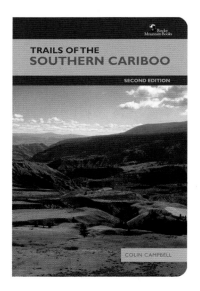

Trails of the Southern Cariboo
Second Edition

Colin Campbell

Surrounded by the historic remnants of the Gold Rush, with a tiny population and a huge landmass comprising a variety of subregions and topographies, the south-central region of the British Columbia interior's trails have always been famous for great hiking.

In this completely revised, updated and full-colour edition, residents and tourists alike will learn about and experience both traditional hiking and cross-country ski trails of varying lengths and terrain. The diverse routes in this dynamic region include stunning meadow trails, occasional breathtaking scrambles and numerous longer hikes.

ISBN 978-1-897522-44-8

Colour Photos, Maps

$19.95, softcover

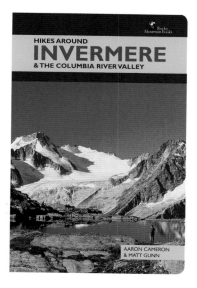

Hikes around Invermere
& the Columbia River Valley

Aaron Cameron & Matt Gunn

Located in the southeast corner of British Columbia, the Windermere Valley is at the headwaters of the mighty Columbia. The ideal base for exploring this spectacular country of the northern Purcells and the western slopes of the Canadian Rockies is the picturesque town of Invermere.

From short strolls to dayhikes to overnighters to major, committing mountaineering routes, this book has all the information you need to get out there and enjoy the most beautiful spots at Spillimacheen River, Horsethief, Toby and Frances creeks and Mount Assiniboine as well as in the Stanford Range, the Bugaboos, Kootenay National Park and Height of the Rockies.

ISBN 978-1-897522-51-6

Colour and Black & White Photos, Maps

$19.95, softcover

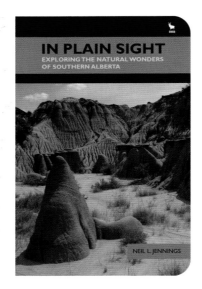

IN PLAIN SIGHT
Exploring the Natural Wonders of Southern Alberta

Neil L. Jennings

In Plain Sight highlights a selection of natural wonders and outdoor adventures located in southern Alberta. The places featured in this book have been chosen for their utter uniqueness, beauty and splendour. Some are easy to get to and easy to get around in; others require a bit more time and energy. Overall, you will be stimulated, enlightened, delighted, amazed, uplifted and broadened by the experience. These are truly awesome places, in the very real meaning of that word. All are in plain sight, though they are little visited by locals or tourists.

ISBN 978-1-897522-78-3
Colour Photos, Maps
$26.95, Softcover

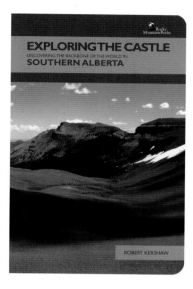

EXPLORING THE CASTLE

Discovering the Backbone of the World in Southern Alberta

Robert Kershaw

In 1901, naturalist George Bird Grinnell took note of an extensive network of mountains, ridges, valleys, lakes and rivers on both sides of the Continental Divide from northern Montana into southern British Columbia and Alberta. Disregarding political boundaries, he named it "The Crown of the Continent." While "Crown of the Continent" speaks eloquently of the region's beauty with more than a passing nod to European monarchy and history, the Blackfoot name carries a more vital and universal meaning: "Mo'kakiikin," the "backbone of the world." At the heart of this complex landscape lies the Castle Wilderness.

ISBN 978-1-897522-04-2

Colour Photos, Maps

$26.95, Softcover

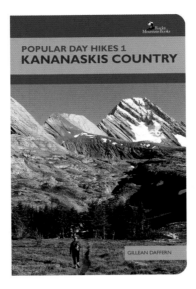

Popular Day Hikes 1
Kananaskis Country

Gillean Daffern

This is a book of popular day hikes in one of southern Alberta's most-loved outdoor recreation areas. Kananaskis Country covers more than 4,000 square kilometres of the Canadian Rockies south and east of Banff National Park, and is a favourite destination for outdoors enthusiasts of all ages and abilities. This book features 34 hikes, with detailed descriptions focusing on quality trails with easy access and good staging areas. Factual and informative, *Popular Day Hikes 1* is complete with maps and colour photographs and is sure to satisfy locals and visitors alike.

ISBN 978-1-894765-90-9

Colour Photos, Maps

$15.95, Softcover

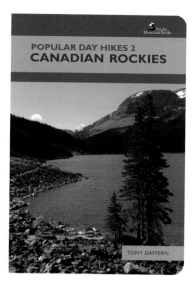

Popular Day Hikes 2
Canadian Rockies

Tony Daffern

Following up on the success of the first book in the Popular Day Hikes series - Gillean Daffern's *Popular Day Hikes 1: Kananaskis Country* - Rocky Mountain Books is thrilled to offer this companion volume focusing on the splendour of the Canadian Rockies. The Popular Day Hikes series is written for visitors and locals looking to hike scenic trails from well-established staging areas. These factual, attractive guides feature detailed maps and colour photographs throughout.

ISBN 978-1-897522-01-1
Colour Photos, Maps
$15.95, Softcover

LIFE OF THE TRAIL 1 HISTORIC HIKES IN
EASTERN BANFF NATIONAL PARK

EMERSON SANFORD &
JANICE SANFORD BECK

ISBN 978-1-894765-99-2

Colour and Black & White Photos, Maps

$26.95 NOW $22.95, Softcover

LIFE OF THE TRAIL 2 HISTORIC HIKES IN
NORTHERN YOHO NATIONAL PARK

EMERSON SANFORD &
JANICE SANFORD BECK

ISBN 978-1-897522-00-4

Colour and Black & White Photos, Maps

$26.95 NOW $22.95, Softcover

LIFE OF THE TRAIL 3 THE HISTORIC ROUTE
FROM OLD BOW FORT TO JASPER

EMERSON SANFORD &
JANICE SANFORD BECK

ISBN 978-1-897522-41-7

Colour and Black & White Photos, Maps

$26.95 NOW $22.95, Softcover

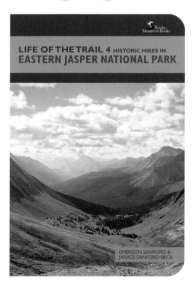

LIFE OF THE TRAIL 4 HISTORIC HIKES IN
EASTERN JASPER NATIONAL PARK

EMERSON SANFORD &
JANICE SANFORD BECK

ISBN 978-1-897522-42-2

Colour and Black & White Photos, Maps

$26.95 NOW $22.95, Softcover

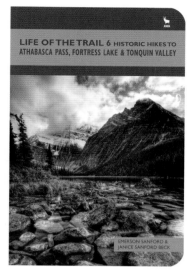

ISBN 978-1-897522-80-6

Colour and Black & White Photos, Maps

$26.95 NOW $22.95, Softcover

ISBN 978-1-926855-24-0

Colour and Black & White Photos, Maps

$26.95 NOW $22.95, Softcover

LIFE OF THE TRAIL

Emerson Sanford & Janice Sanford Beck

When authors Emerson Sanford and Janice Sanford Beck began back-packing together nearly 20 years ago, they often wondered whose footsteps they were retracing and how today's Rockies trails came to be there. In the Life of the Trail series, they share their findings with hikers and history buffs, adventurers and armchair travellers.

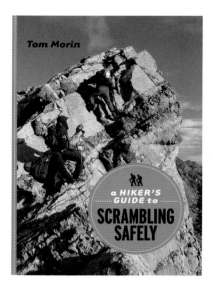

A Hiker's Guide to Scrambling Safely

Tom Morin

Unroped scrambling over so-called easy terrain is one of the most potentially dangerous recreational activities. Every year, scramblers are injured or killed in preventable accidents. *A Hiker's Guide to Scrambling Safely* educates new scramblers in the inherent risks and required climbing skills and imparts the mountaineering knowledge necessary for safety when the going gets steep.

ISBN 978-1-894765-66-4
Black & White Photos
$14.95, Softcover

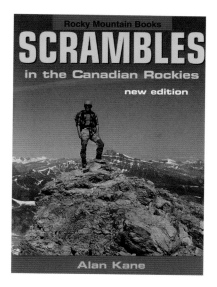

SCRAMBLES

In the Canadian Rockies

Alan Kane

Scrambles is completely revised and updated with over 50 new scrambles and 156 easy peaks with a wide range of difficulty suitable for novice climbers and experienced hikers who want a little more challenge. Illustrated with 188 route photos.

ISBN 978-0-921102-67-0
Black & White Photos
$29.95, Softcover